WHOOPS

This is the back of the book!

Manga Classics™ books follow the Japanese comic (aka Manga!) reading order. Traditional manga is read in a "reversed" format starting on the right and heading towards the left. The story begins where English readers expect to find the last page because the spine of the book is on the opposite side. Flip to the other end of the book and start reading your Manga Classics!

S0-BSA-819

Adventures of
HUCKLEBERRY
FINN
MARK TWAIN

Art by: Kuma Chan
Story Adaptation by: Crystal S. Chan
Lettering: Jeannie Lee

STAFF:

Project Chief North America: Erik Ko
Editor: M. Chandler
VP of Sales: John Shableski
Project Manager: Janice Leung
Copy Editing Assistant: Michelle Lee

Project Chief Asia: Andy Hung
Production Manager: Yuen Him Tai
Art Assistants: Man Yiu, Shirley Yuen
Calvin, Touyu, VIP96neko
Shougo, Ron, Stoon

AGE: Young Adult (12+)
BISAC: YAF010060 YAF010010 YAF009000 YAF010000
YOUNG ADULT FICTION, Comics & Graphic Novels, Manga, Classic Adaptation
DEWEY: FIC
SUBJECT CATEGORIES: Comics/Graphic Novels/Manga,Fiction General Adventure,
Humor, Social Commentary, Antebellum South, Slavery

First Printing September 2017   Printer in Canada
HARD COVER EDITION   ISBN # 978-1-772940-16-9   PAPERBACK EDITION   ISBN # 978-1-772940-17-6

w w w . m a n g a c l a s s i c s . c o m

Manga Classics™

Manga Classics™ proudly presents:
the finest name in adaptations of beloved classic literature!

Manga Classics, Inc. is proud to bring you this very special new line of books, adapting classic literature with the same quality and attention to detail as our fantastic graphic novels, art books, and manga releases! This Manga Classics line is the result of an ambitious international partnership with various fine artists in Japan, Korea, and Hong Kong, the aim of which is to bring the highest-quality adaptations of these works to the North American market!

The creative team has worked tirelessly to fully realize the rich worlds of these classic works of literature. Our artists have extensively researched the settings of these timeless novels in order to give the costumes and architecture a very real sense of weight and accuracy, expertly executed thanks to the studio's animation background. This high-quality work has been coupled with a generous page count of over 300 pages per book, more than double the average comics-format adaptation! This allows for more thorough, accurate, and natural adaptations of the source material, with the artists' vision given as much space as needed to be properly realized. In short, all Manga Classics adaptations look and read like great commercial manga while also being faithful adaptations of literary classics!

Intended for a young adult audience, Manga Classics are just as likely to be enjoyed in the reader's free time as in the classroom. The gripping stories and lush artwork easily place them alongside today's best-selling popular manga, with strong and accurate adaptations that are sure to please even the toughest teacher or librarian! Our books are also the perfect way for adult readers to rediscover their favorite classics – or experience them for the first time!

Now that you have read Adventures of Huckleberry Finn, look for Manga Classics adaptations of other classic literature in stores!

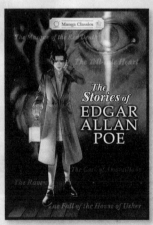

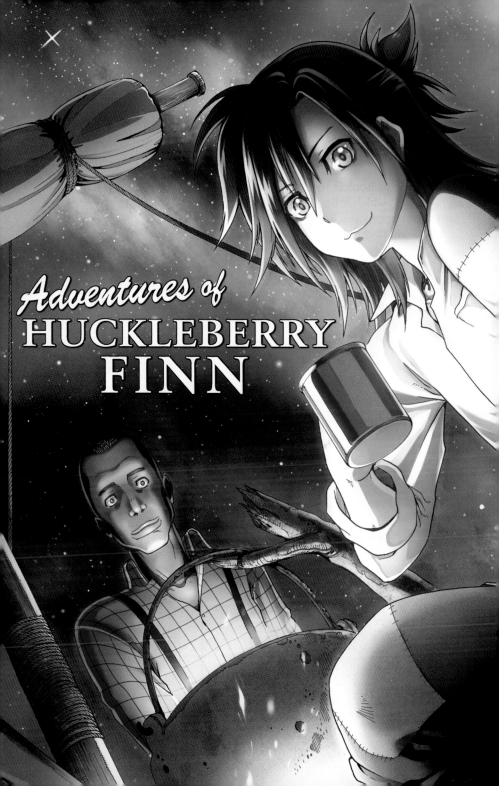

Adventures of
HUCKLEBERRY
FINN

HOW TO READ MANGA!

Hello there, and welcome to **Manga Classics**! "Manga" is a style of comic book originating in **Japan**.

A manga book is read from **right-to-left**, which is **backwards** from the normal books you know. This means that you will find the first page where you expect to find the last page! It also means that each page begins in the top right corner.

START HERE!

2

3

1

If you have never read a manga book before, here is a helpful guide to get you started!

5

4

10

9

6

7

8

Don't forget that each comic panel also reads from **right-to-left!** Here is a single panel:

START HERE!

3

1

2

Now, let's look at reading two pages together!

START HERE!

10 9 8

11

12

15 14 13

16

3

4

1

2

5

6

7

When you get here, go to the next page!

Got the hang of it? Then you're ready to start reading **Manga Classics!**

CONTENTS:

Publisher's Note:

We tried to keep the chapter breaks from the original novel.

However, because of the adaptation process, sometimes we had to combine a few chapters.

Those chapters are listed as combined.

FOREWORD

Adventures of Huckleberry Finn has often been criticized, expurgated and banned since its publication in 1884. Although the novel is best known for its extensive use of coarse language and racial stereotypes, it was originally intended to be a scathing satire on historically entrenched attitudes regarding class and race.

For this *Manga Classics* edition, we tried to preserve as much of Mark Twain's original language as possible to uphold the historical integrity of the work. By exposing rather than burying the past, this *Manga Classics* version aims to help students think critically about current racial slurs and stereotypes by tracing them back to their historical origins, and examining the intent and viewpoints of those associated with them.

The root of the Common Core State Standards is to teach students how to read thoughtfully, think critically and engage with literary texts. In order to do this, educators need to address the language, power and history of race relations in the United States — far beyond simply bowdlerizing parts of a work that may stir up student racial insensitivity and teacher discomfort.

Whereas removing racially objectionable content may alleviate some discomfort, from an educational standpoint the practice can be viewed as counterproductive. Societal discomfort is oftentimes a clear indication that our current values and beliefs are being challenged in a way that moves us, enabling us to truly engage with a piece of literature. Understanding Twain's novel goes beyond comprehending the story's plot. It involves coming to terms with our country's racist past as we experience the complex racial dynamics of Twain's Mississippi.

In actuality, Twain was a progressive leader whose racial politics were decades ahead of his time. His use of coarse vernacular and racial stereotypes in the novel was intended not to endorse but rather to ridicule the racism of his day. This *Manga Classics* version of *Adventures of Huckleberry Finn* is presented as a way for contemporary readers to engage with and consider multiple perspectives from our nation's historical past and to examine it in light of our current values. I hope you enjoy this artistic interpretation of one of the most colorful and engaging literary works in American history.

Julie Vo, M.Ed.
Associate Dean
Stanford University Alumni

EXPLANATORY

IN this book a number of dialects are used, to wit: the Missouri negro dialect; the extremest form of the backwoods Southwestern dialect; the ordinary "Pike County" dialect; and four modified varieties of this last. The shadings have not been done in a haphazard fashion, or by guesswork; but painstakingly, and with the trustworthy guidance and support of personal familiarity with these several forms of speech.

I make this explanation for the reason that without it many readers would suppose that all these characters were trying to talk alike and not succeeding.

THE AUTHOR.

THE MID-1840S
THE SMALL MISSISSIPPI RIVER TOWN OF ST. PETERSBURGH, MISSOURI, USA

MY NAME'S HUCKLEBERRY FINN, ALTHOUGH MOST PEOPLE CALLS ME HUCK.

CHAPTER-I

YOU DON'T KNOW ABOUT ME WITHOUT YOU HAVE READ A BOOK BY THE NAME OF THE ADVENTURES OF TOM SAWYER; BUT THAT AIN'T NO MATTER.

THAT BOOK WAS MADE BY MR. MARK TWAIN, AND HE TOLD THE TRUTH, MAINLY.

THERE WERE SOME THINGS HE STRETCHED BUT MAINLY HE TOLD THE TRUTH.

NOW THE WAY THAT BOOK WINDS UP IS THIS: TOM AND ME FOUND THE MONEY THAT THE ROBBERS HID IN THE CAVE, AND IT MADE US RICH. WE GOT SIX THOUSAND DOLLARS APIECE - ALL GOLD.

WELL, JUDGE THATCHER HE TOOK IT AND PUT IT OUT AT INTEREST, AND IT FETCHED US A DOLLAR A DAY APIECE ALL THE YEAR ROUND - MORE THAN A BODY COULD TELL WHAT TO DO WITH.

THE WIDOW DOUGLAS SHE TOOK ME FOR HER SON, AND ALLOWED SHE WOULD SIVILIZE ME, AS SHE WAS REGULAR AND DECENT IN ALL HER WAYS.

IT WAS AN AWFUL SIGHT OF MONEY WHEN IT WAS PILED UP!

SHE WAS GOOD TO ME, AND FRIENDLY.

BUT...

8

I'VE TRIED IT, AND IT DON'T WORK; IT AIN'T FOR ME!

BUT I CAN'T BEAR IT!

WHEN SHE RANG A BELL FOR SUPPER, YOU HAD TO BE THERE ON TIME - WHEN YOU WERE AT THE TABLE YOU COULDN'T EAT UNTIL SHE TUCKED DOWN HER HEAD AND GRUMBLED OVER THE FOOD... BEING RESPECTABLE AIN'T WHAT IT'S CRACKED UP TO BE. IT'S JUST WORRY AND WORRY.

SHE WAS JUST TOO RESPECTABLE AND DECENT - SHE FORCED ME TO WEAR ALL THESE CUSSED SMOTHERY THINGS AND TAKE BATHS. SHE DIDN'T MEAN NO HARM, BUT I COULDN'T STAND IT!

AND HER SISTER, MISS WATSON! SHE WAS WORSE!

THIS OLD MAID WAS ALWAYS AT ME, WORKING ME HARD UNTIL THE WIDOW MADE HER EASE UP.

...er Which Art In Heaven, Hallowed be...

I COULDN'T EVEN SCRATCH OR STRETCH WITHOUT HER PICKING ON ME, ALWAYS ASKING WHY I COULDN'T BEHAVE.

SHE SAID THAT ONLY PEOPLE WHO BEHAVED CAN GO TO THE GOOD PLACE.

I DON'T WANT TO GO TO MISS WATSON'S PROVIDENCE! ALL A BODY WOULD HAVE TO DO THERE IS PLAY WITH THE HARP AND SING – I DON'T THINK MUCH OF THAT.

THE GOOD PLACE THE WIDOW DOUGLAS TALKED ABOUT MADE MY MOUTH WATER, THOUGH. IT SOUNDED A LOT NICER.

I ASKED IF SHE RECKONED TOM SAWYER WOULD GO THERE. SHE SAID, NOT BY A CONSIDERABLE SIGHT.

I RECKON A POOR CHAP WOULD STAND CONSIDERABLE SHOW WITH THE WIDOW'S PROVIDENCE.

I'M GLAD ABOUT THAT, BECAUSE I WANT HIM AND ME TO BE TOGETHER.

STILL, I RECKONED I'D BELONG TO THE WIDOW'S IF HE WANTED ME, THOUGH I COULDN'T MAKE OUT HOW HE WAS GOING TO BE BETTER OFF.

COURSE, IF MISS WATSON'S PROVIDENCE GOT HIM THERE WARN'T NO HELP FOR HIM ANY MORE.

10

I PRAYED THREE OR FOUR TIMES, ON MY KNEES LIKE HOW THE WIDOW SHOWED ME, BUT I NEVER GOT THAT FISH-HOOK THAT I WANTED.

MISS WATSON TOLD ME TO PRAY EVERY DAY, AND WHATEVER I ASKED FOR I WOULD GET IT. BUT IT WARN'T SO.

THE WIDOW TOLD ME WHAT I COULD GET WERE "SPIRITUAL GIFTS". WELL, THAT WON'T DO ME MUCH GOOD!

MISS WATSON SHE KEPT PECKING AT ME, AND IT GOT TIRESOME.

I KEPT TRYING TO THINK OF SOMETHING CHEERFUL, BUT IT WARN'T NO USE. I FELT SO LONESOME I MOST WISH I WAS DEAD.

AROOOOO

RUSTLE RUSTLE

WHOO-WHOOOOOO

SHHHHHH

OWL AWAY OFF, CRYING ABOUT SOMEBODY THAT'S DEAD...

THAT'S MOST LIKE THE SOUND A GHOST MAKES WHEN IT CAN'T MAKE ITSELF UNDERSTOOD...

I'M AWFUL SCARED - WISH I HAD SOME COMPANY.

!

STTTTT

STTT

WHAP

KILLING A SPIDER - THAT'S AN AWFUL BAD SIGN!

TURN AROUND IN MY TRACKS THREE TIMES, CROSS MY CHEST EVERY TIME...

TIE UP SOME HAIR TO KEEP THE WITCHES AWAY...

I HAIN'T GOT NO CONFIDENCE IN IT, THOUGH.

THAT AIN'T ANY WAY TO KEEP OFF THE BAD LUCK WHEN YOU'VE KILLED A SPIDER.

TWIRL

UGH! I CAN'T BEAR THIS – NOW IT'S ALL STILL OUT THERE.

STILLER THAN EVER – I HEARD THE CLOCK AWAY OFF IN TOWN, TWELVE LICKS –

I'M STILL A-SHAKING ALL OVER – WHERE IS TOM, ANYHOW?

THERE HE IS!

ME-YOW!

ME-YOW!

!

WHY DO I GOT TO CLIMB OUT OF MY WINDOW LIKE A BURGLAR?

BURGLAR! YOU AIN'T THAT CHEAP!

SHUF

SHUF

TMP

ONCE YOU JOIN THE GANG YOU'LL BE A REAL ROBBER.

ROBBERS HAVE GOT MORE STYLE THAN PLAIN BURGLARS!

LET'S GO, THEN!

TOM SAWYER

ZZN

HANG ON! SOMEONE'S THERE!

CHAPTER II & CHAPTER III

!

IS IT JIM?

MISS WATSON'S BIG NIGGER?

WE NEEDS TO GO. HE MIGHT MAKE A DISTURBANCE, AND IF HE DID THAT THEY'D FIND OUT I WARN'T IN.

!

?!

THUD

HEY! WHO DAH?

SAY, WHO IS YOU? WHAR IS YOU?

...

DOG MY CATS EF I DIDN'T HEAR SUMF'N.

...

I'S GWYNE TO SET DOWN HERE AND LISTEN TELL I HEARS IT AGIN.

WELL, I KNOW WHAT I'S GWYNE TO DO:

18

ZZZ

UGH... I ITCH ALL OVER... IN UPWARDS OF A THOUSAND PLACES... I DASSEN'T SCRATCH!

HE'S ASLEEP?!

PROBABLY HE'S BEEN WAITING FOR TOO LONG.

LET'S GET OUT OF HERE!

DON'T PUSH ME!

MIGHT BE FUN TO TIE HIM TO THE TREE.

NO! HE MIGHT WAKE.

...

HEY!

ANYWAY, WE DON'T HAVE ENOUGH CANDLES! I'VE GOT TO SNEAK TO THE KITCHEN TO FETCH A FEW – I'LL BE BACK!

AW, I JUST HUNG HIS HAT ON A BRANCH.

I'M BACK! LET'S GO.

WHAT'D YOU DO WITH JIM?

...

ZZZ

DID HE CATCH YOU?

OF COURSE NOT! YOU DON'T SEE HIM COMING AFTER ME.

THIS WAS WIDELY SPREAD AMONG THE NIGGERS – JIM BECAME THE MOST RESPECTED FELLOW IN THE AREA, AND HE GOT TO BE MONSTROUS PROUD ABOUT IT.

AFTERWARDS JIM SAID THAT THE WITCHES BEWITCHED HIM AND PUT HIM IN A TRANCE, AND RODE HIM ALL OVER THE STATE.

THEY EVEN HUNG HIS HAT ON THE BRANCH OF THE TREE TO SHOW WHO DONE IT.

WE WENT DOWN THE HILL AND FOUND JO HARPER AND BEN ROGERS, AND TWO OR THREE MORE OF THE BOYS.

TOM AND ME GOT TO THE EDGE OF THE HILL-TOP AND THE STARS OVER US WAS SPARKLING EVER SO FINE.

WE UNHITCHED A SKIFF AND PULLED DOWN THE RIVER TWO MILE AND A HALF, TO THE BIG SCAR ON THE HILLSIDE, AND WENT ASHORE.

WE'LL START THIS BAND OF ROBBERS AND CALL IT TOM SAWYER'S GANG!

STICK TO THE OATH THAT YOU TOOK – IF YOU TELL ANYONE OUR SECRETS, YOU'LL BE KILLED!

YES!

IT'S A REAL BEAUTIFUL OATH, TOM.

HAHA! I THOUGHT UP SOME OF IT, BUT THE REST WAS OUT OF PIRATE-BOOKS AND ROBBER-BOOKS.

EVERY HIGH-TONED GANG HAS ONE LIKE IT!

WOULDN'T IT BE GOOD TO KILL THE *FAMILIES* OF BOYS WHO TELL THE SECRETS, TOO?

GOOD IDEA! I'LL WRITE IT IN.

HE HAIN'T GOT NO FAMILY; WHAT ARE YOU GOING TO DO 'BOUT HIM?

WHAT 'BOUT HUCK?

AH!

WELL, HAIN'T HE GOT A FATHER?

YES, HE'S GOT A FATHER...

... BUT YOU CAN'T NEVER FIND HIM THESE DAYS.

HE USED TO LAY DRUNK WITH THE HOGS IN THE TANYARD, BUT HE HAIN'T BEEN SEEN IN THESE PARTS FOR A YEAR OR MORE.

ALL OF US HAVE A FAMILY – ONLY HUCK DON'T HAVE ANYBODY TO KILL. IT HAIN'T FAIR.

I'M GLAD MY PAP AIN'T AROUND NO MORE, BUT I DON'T WANT TO GET KICKED OUT OF TOM SAWYER'S GANG BECAUSE OF IT!

BUT WE ALL WANT HUCK TO JOIN US, RIGHT?

THEY'RE GOING TO RULE ME OUT IF THEY CAN'T THINK OF ANYTHING TO DO...

AS LONG AS HUCK'S FATHER SHOWS UP, WE CAN KILL HIM.

BUT WHAT IF HE DON'T SHOW UP?

IT'S TRUE – BUT BEN'S RIGHT. IT'D BE UNFAIR TO THE OTHERS.

EH...

THEY WAS STUMPED, AND I WAS MOST READY TO CRY –

OH! HOW ABOUT MISS WATSON? YOU CAN KILL HER.

OH, SHE'LL DO.

HUCK CAN COME IN.

!

SO IT WORKS?

HOORAY!

MUST WE ALWAYS KILL THE PEOPLE?

OH, CERTAINLY. IT'S BEST. UNLESS WE LOCK THEM IN THE CAVE AND HOLD THEM 'TIL THEY'RE RANSOMED.

WHAT'S THE LINE OF BUSINESS OF THIS GANG?

NOTHING ONLY ROBBERY AND MURDER!

WE'RE HIGHWAYMEN! WE PUT ON MASKS AND KILL THE PEOPLE ON THE ROAD FOR THEIR MONEY!

!

RANSOMED? WHAT'S THAT?

I DON'T KNOW. BUT THAT'S WHAT THEY DO IN THE BOOKS.

EVERYONE! LISTEN TO ME! I GOT SOME SECRET NEWS I JUST REMEMBERED!

WE CAN ROB US TWO HUNDRED ELEPHANTS AND SIX HUNDRED CAMELS TOMORROW!

PERFECT! WHO'S GOT THEM?

JO HARPER

WE'LL ATTACK FROM AMBUSH TOMORROW, AND WE'LL KILL THE LOT AND SCOOP THE THINGS!

GOOD! THIS IS THE OPPORTUNITY FOR "TOM SAWYER'S GANG" TO GET FAMOUS!

THERE'S A WHOLE PARCEL OF SPANISH MERCHANTS THAT'S GONNA CAMP IN CAVE HOLLOW. THEY ONLY HAVE FOUR HUNDRED GUARDS!

YES!

LET'S POLISH THE GUNS AND SWORDS!

SHUF

SHUF

BUT I WANT TO SEE THE ELEPHANTS AND THE CAMELS...

BUT... I DON'T BELIEVE WE COULD REALLY LICK FOUR HUNDRED SOLDIERS. AND AIN'T THESE GUNS AND SWORDS STILL TRASH AND BROOMSTICKS NO MATTER HOW HARD WE POLISH?

WE'VE GOT TO GET THEM SCOURED AND READY!

HOPE THE WEATHER WILL BE NICE TOMORROW...

AND OF COURSE THERE WARN'T NO MERCHANTS NOR GUARDS, AND THERE WARN'T NO ELEPHANTS NOR CAMELS -

- BUT ONLY A SUNDAY-SCHOOL PICNIC, AND A PRIMER-CLASS AT THAT.

WE NEVER GOT ANYTHING BUT THEIR DONUTS AND JAM, AND WE HAD TO DROP EVERYTHING AND CUT WHEN THE TEACHER CAME CHARGING IN.

KILL THEM!

ROB THEM!

BUT TOM SAID LATER THAT THERE WERE MERCHANTS AND JEWELS THERE ALL ALONG, AND I'D KNOW THAT WITHOUT ASKING IF I'D READ A BOOK CALLED "DON QUIXOTE".

AND THEY'D FOOLED US BY TURNING THE MERCHANTS INTO AN INFANT SUNDAY SCHOOL BY ENCHANTMENT. JUST FOR SPITE.

OUR ENEMIES HAD BEEN MAGICIANS

I THOUGHT THAT MEANT WE SHOULD KILL THE MAGICIANS, THEN – BUT TOM SAID THEY'D JUST SUMMON GENIES TO BEAT US UP INSTEAD.

HE TRIED TO EXPLAIN ABOUT GENIES BUT IT DIDN'T MAKE MUCH SENSE, WITH ALL THE RUBBING LAMPS AND RINGS AND SUCH.

WE PLAYED AT BEING ROBBERS NOW AND THEN ABOUT A MONTH AND THEN EVERYONE RESIGNED.

I RECKON HE BELIEVED THEY WERE MERCHANTS AND ELEPHANTS,

BUT AS FOR ME I THINK DIFFERENT. IT HAD ALL THE MARKS OF A SUNDAY-SCHOOL.

WE HADN'T ROBBED NOBODY, HADN'T KILLED ANY PEOPLE, BUT ONLY JUST PRETENDED.

CHAPTER IV

HOUSE OF WIDOW DOUGLAS

AFTER THREE OR FOUR MONTHS, I GOT TO WHERE I COULD STAND LIVING WITH THE WIDOW AND GOING TO SCHOOL..

BUT I KNOCKED OVER THE SALT-CELLAR THIS MORNING. THAT'S SOME BAD LUCK...

HFF

HFF

THAT'S CURIOUS. WHAT WAS HE DOING?

EH? WHY ARE THERE FOOTSTEPS IN THE SNOW? WHO LEFT THE TRACKS?

FUNNY HE DIDN'T COME IN, AFTER STANDING AROUND SO...

!

A CROSS MADE FROM NAILS ON THE HEEL OF HIS LEFT BOOT?

THIS CROSS IS MEANT TO KEEP OFF THE DEVIL... WHERE HAVE I SEEN THIS BEFORE?

NO! I CAN'T LET HIM GET MY MONEY!

HOUSE OF JUDGE THATCHER

SLAM

JUDGE THATCHER

?

WHY, MY BOY, YOU ARE ALL OUT OF BREATH.

DID YOU COME FOR YOUR INTEREST?

NO, SIR, I DIDN'T.

I WANT TO GIVE IT TO YOU — THE SIX THOUSAND AND ALL.

WELL, I'M PUZZLED.

DON'T YOU ASK ME NO QUESTIONS ABOUT IT, PLEASE.

YOU'LL TAKE IT - WON'T YOU?

WHY, WHAT CAN YOU MEAN, MY BOY?

IS SOMETHING THE MATTER?

PLEASE TAKE IT.

AND DON'T ASK ME NOTHING - THEN I WON'T HAVE TO TELL NO LIES.

...

OHO-O!

I THINK I SEE.

THAT'S THE CORRECT IDEA.

YOU WANT TO SELL ALL YOUR PROPERTY TO ME - NOT GIVE IT.

RIGHT.

SO I SOLD ALL MY PROPERTY TO JUDGE THATCHER, AND HE GIVE ME A DOLLAR FOR IT.

THE SAME NIGHT

HOUSE OF WIDOW DOUGLAS

IF PAP CAME BACK FOR MY MONEY, AT LEAST HE CAN'T GET IT...

JIM DID A MAGIC SPELL TO SEE AND SAW TWO ANGELS HOVERING BY MY FATHER'S HEAD –

A WHITE ANGEL THAT WOULD GET HIM TO ACT RIGHT FOR A WHILE AND A BLACK ANGEL THAT WOULD SAIL IN AND BUST IT ALL UP –

THAT I SHOULD REST EASY AND LET HIM MAKE HIS OWN WAY...

I CAN'T JUST REST EASY!

WHAT'S PAP AIMING TO DO?

CHAPTER V TO VII

HA! STARCHY CLOTHES – VERY.

SO, HE CAME HERE...

!

YOU THINK YOU'RE A GOOD DEAL OF A BIG-BUG, DON'T YOU?

AFTER THE FIRST SHOCK, I KNEW THAT I WASN'T SCARED OF HIM NO MORE.

MAYBE I AM, MAYBE I AIN'T.

YOU'RE EDUCATED, TOO, THEY SAY. YOU THINK YOU'RE BETTER'N YOUR FATHER, NOW, DON'T YOU.

HE MUST HAVE CLIMBED IN THROUGH THAT WINDOW...

DON'T YOU GIVE ME NONE O' YOUR LIP!

YOU'VE PUT ON CONSIDERABLE MANY FRILLS SINCE I BEEN AWAY!

I'LL TAKE YOU DOWN A PEG BEFORE I GET DONE WITH YOU!

WELL, I'LL LEARN HER HOW TO MEDDLE.

WHO TOLD YOU YOU MIGHT MEDDLE WITH SUCH HIFALUT'N FOOLISHNESS, HEY?

THE WIDOW. SHE TOLD ME.

I AIN'T THE MAN TO STAND IT—YOU HEAR?

I NEVER SEEN SUCH A SON!

WHAT'S THIS?

!

IT'S SOMETHING THEY GIVE ME FOR LEARNING MY LESSONS GOOD.

RIIIIIP

I'LL GIVE YOU SOMETHING BETTER -

I'LL GIVE YOU A COWHIDE.

THEY SAY YOU'RE RICH. HEY? - HOW'S THAT?

THAT'S WHY I COME. YOU GIT ME THAT MONEY TO-MORROW - I WANT IT.

THEY LIE - THAT'S HOW.

I AIN'T GOT NO MONEY.

YOU CAN'T TRICK ME.

IT'S A LIE!

I AIN'T GOT NO MONEY.

JUDGE THATCHER'S GOT IT. YOU GIT IT. I WANT IT!

YOU ASK JUDGE THATCHER; HE'LL TELL YOU THE SAME.

GO ON, THEN.

ALL RIGHT. I'LL ASK HIM.

THE NEXT DAY PAP GOT DRUNK AND HE WENT TO JUDGE THATCHER'S AND BULLYRAGGED HIM, TRYING TO MAKE HIM GIVE UP THE MONEY, BUT HE COULDN'T.

SO PAP SWORE HE'D MAKE THE LAW FORCE HIM.

UNFORTUNATELY THE NEW JUDGE DIDN'T KNOW HOW THE OLD MAN WAS, SO HE RULED AGAINST IT.

AT THE SAME TIME, JUDGE THATCHER AND THE WIDOW TRIED TO GET THE LAW TO TAKE ME AWAY FROM PAP AND LET ONE OF THEM TO BE MY GUARDIAN.

THAT PLEASED THE OLD MAN, BUT HE WAS BITTER, TOO, BECAUSE OF THE MONEY.

PAP CAME TO THE WIDOW'S HOUSE TO BOTHER ME, AND HE TRIED TO KEEP ME AWAY FROM SCHOOL. FINALLY THE WIDOW COULDN'T BEAR IT NO MORE.

42

SHE WARNED HIM THAT SHE WAS GOING TO MAKE TROUBLE FOR HIM, AND *WASN'T* HE MAD!

ALTHOUGH I DIDN'T WANT TO GO TO SCHOOL MUCH, I RECKONED I'D KEEP GOING JUST TO SPITE HIM.

SOME SPRING DAY, AFTER SCHOOL

MY FATHER JUST WON'T STOP GOING AFTER THAT MONEY.

PAP MUST BE IN A BAD MOOD. I'LL BORROW TWO OR THREE DOLLARS FROM JUDGE THATCHER FOR HIM TO BUY WHISKEY WITH.

AND THIS LAW BUSINESS IS AWFUL SLOW...

IF HE DON'T GET HIS WHISKEY I'LL GET A COWHIDING...

MMF!

JO WANTS TO SKIP CLASS AND HAVE SOME FUN. YOU COMING, HUCK?

HUCK? WHERE ARE YOU?

HE WAS JUST HERE.

EH?

SIIIGH

TWO MONTHS LATER

CATCH ANYTHING?

NOT YET.

THEN GET BACK IN THE HOUSE!

ALTHOUGH PAP KEPT ME LOCKED UP AND I NEVER GOT A CHANCE TO RUN OFF,

I DIDN'T HAVE TO GO TO SCHOOL, OR FOLLOW THE RULES, OR WASH AND COMB UP – IT WARN'T SO BAD.

HE GOT SO HE WAS HITTING ME TOO MUCH, AND I COULDN'T STAND IT.

EXCEPT...

UGH!

46

HURRY AND GET IN!

GOING TO THE STORE TO TRADE FOR WHISKEY AGAIN?

GOT NOTHING TO DO WITH YOU!

AIN'T YOUR BUSINESS!

HOW'S IT NOT MY BUSINESS? WHENEVER YOU GET DRUNK YOU BEAT ON ME!

THUD

MOSTLY WHEN PAP GOT DRUNK HE WOULD ONLY CUSS THE GOVMENT UP ONE SIDE AND DOWN THE OTHER, RIPPING ON HOW HE WAS WORTH SIX THOUSAND DOLLARS AND STILL COULDN'T GET HIS RIGHTS...

LAST TIME, THOUGH, HE GOT WILD AND CHASED ME ROUND AND ROUND THE PLACE WITH A CLASP-KNIFE, FIGURING I WAS THE ANGEL OF DEATH!

HUFF

HUFF

MIGHT NOT BE SO LUCKY, NEXT TIME.

I GOT AWAY THAT TIME BY PURE LUCK.

HE GOT TO GOING AWAY A LOT, TOO, AND LOCKING ME IN.

CLICK

IF ONE DAY HE DON'T COME BACK, I'LL BE DEAD FOR SURE!

I MADE UP MY MIND TO RUN AWAY.

I MADE A HOLE UNDER THE WALL SO THAT I COULD CRAWL OUT WHILE PAP WAS AWAY.

BUT THAT WARN'T GOING TO BE ENOUGH TO KEEP HIM FROM COMING AFTER ME.

SO I TOOK THE AXE AND SMASHED IN THE DOOR,

I TOOK AN OLD SACK AND FILLED IT WITH ROCKS, DRAGGING IT FROM WHERE THE PIG WAS ALL THE WAY TO THE RIVER, SO THAT YOU COULD EASY SEE THAT SOMETHING HAD BEEN DRAGGED OVER THE GROUND AND DUMPED INTO THE RIVER.

LAST I CUT A HOLE IN A SACK OF CORNMEAL, AND MADE A LITTLE TRACK OF CORNMEAL ALL THE WAY TO THE LAKE, LIKE SOMEONE HAD TORN THE SACK BY ACCIDENT.

THEN I DUMPED THE DEAD PIG IN AFTER.

THEN I SHOT A WILD PIG AND DRAGGED HIM INTO THE CABIN AND LAID HIM DOWN ON THE GROUND TO BLEED.

THERE. I HAD MADE A MURDER.

I DID WISH TOM WAS THERE. HE WOULD HAVE TAKEN AN INTEREST IN MY PLAN, AND HE WOULD HAVE KNOWN ALL THE FANCY TOUCHES TO ADD.

NOBODY WAS AS GOOD AS TOM IN SUCH A THING AS THAT.

ONCE I WAS DONE, I TOOK EVERYTHING I COULD AND PUT IT IN A CANOE THAT I'D FOUND AND HID EARLIER.

I WAITED FOR EVENING AND PADDLED AWAY.

THEY'LL THINK I WAS KILLED BY THE ROBBERS WHO TOOK OUR THINGS, AND THEY WON'T EVER HUNT THE RIVER FOR ANYTHING BUT MY CARCASS. THEY'LL GET TIRED OF THAT SOON ENOUGH.

ALL RIGHT. I CAN GO ANYWHERE I WANT TO NOW.

THE MOON HAD ROSE, AND I WAS PRETTY TIRED, AND THE FIRST THING I KNOWED, I WAS ASLEEP...

THE NEXT MORNING

JACKSON'S ISLAND

I'M POWERFUL COMFORTABLE – DON'T WANT TO GET UP AND COOK BREAKFAST YET.

CHAPTER VIII

I KNOW THIS ISLAND PRETTY WELL, AND NOBODY EVER COMES HERE. I CAN PADDLE OVER TO TOWN NIGHTS AND SLINK AROUND. JACKSON'S ISLAND IS GOOD ENOUGH FOR ME.

OH! THERE'S A FERRYBOAT FULL OF PEOPLE FLOATING ON DOWN – I KNOW WHAT'S THE MATTER.

BOOM

CAW

CAW

CAW

NO MATTER HOW MANY CANNONS THEY FIRE, MY CARCASS AIN'T GONNA RISE TO THE SURFACE!

THINK I'LL GO KEEP A LOOKOUT.

PAP, AND JUDGE THATCHER, AND THE WIDOW...

TOM, MARY, AND BECKY, TOO...

EH?

... THEY ALWAYS PUT QUICKSILVER IN LOAVES OF BREAD AND FLOAT THEM OFF, BECAUSE THEY GO RIGHT TO THE DROWNDED CARCASS AND STOP THERE.

EVERYBODY'S TALKING ABOUT THE MURDER! I FOOLED EVERYONE!

I'M NOT DROWNDED, THOUGH... WILL IT STILL COME TO ME?

I'M PRETTY HUNGRY... BUT IT WON'T DO TO START A FIRE. THEY MIGHT SEE THE SMOKE.

IF SOME OF THAT QUICKSILVER BREAD COMES FLOATING AROUND AFTER ME, I'LL GIVE THEM A GOOD SHOW.

HMM?

GRRUUU

SHAKE OUT THE LITTLE DAB OF QUICKSILVER SO I CAN EAT IT...

BREAD!

AND IT'S BAKER'S BREAD, REAL QUALITY! I AM SO LUCKY!

NOW I RECKON THAT THE WIDOW OR THE PARSON PRAYED THAT THIS BREAD WOULD FIND ME

AND HERE IT HAS GONE AND DONE IT, SO THERE AIN'T NO DOUBT THAT THERE'S SOMETHING IN THAT THING.

MNCH

MNCH

BOOM

WELL, THERE'S SOMETHING IN IT WHEN SOMEONE LIKE THE WIDOW PRAYS, BUT IT DON'T WORK FOR SOMEONE LIKE ME.

I KNOWED I WAS ALL RIGHT NOW. NOBODY ELSE WOULD COME A-HUNTING AFTER ME.

I GOT MY TRAPS OUT OF THE CANOE AND MADE ME A NICE CAMP IN THE THICK WOODS.

I CAUGHT CATFISH WHEN I WAS HUNGRY, AND I LISTENED TO THE SOUND OF THE CURRENT AND COUNTED THE STARS WHEN I GOT LONESOME.

AND SO FOR THREE DAYS AND NIGHTS.

I DIDN'T START THIS CAMP FIRE!

THE ASHES ARE STILL SMOKING...

SOMEONE ELSE IS ON THE ISLAND!

WHO IS IT THAT'S HERE?

WHERE'S THIS FELLOW HIDING? BEEN SEARCHING FOR HIM FOR THE WHOLE DAY...

I SUDDENLY WARN'T FEELING VERY BRASH AT ALL.

I CAN'T LIVE THIS WAY. I'LL FIND OUT WHO'S HERE ON THIS ISLAND WITH ME OR BUST.

WHO IS IT?

THERE'S A FIRE AWAY THROUGH THE TREES...

!

CRACK

SNAP

JIM?

TMP

CRACKLE

HELLO, JIM!

DOAN' HURT ME – DON'T! I HAIN'T EVER DONE NO HARM TO A GHOS'. YOU GO EN GIT IN DE RIVER AGAIN.

–!!

EH?

LISTEN! I AIN'T DEAD!

I ALWUZ LIKED DEAD PEOPLE, EN DONE ALL I COULD FOR 'EM.

DOAN' DO NUFFN TO OLE JIM, 'AT 'UZ AWLUZ YO' FREN'.

I AIN'T DEAD.

...

HAIN'T YOU?

DO I LOOK LIKE A GHOST TO YOU?

60

HUCK!

HEY!

YOU KNOW HOW MY PAP ALWAYS BEAT ME, AND HOW HE TOOK ME AWAY AND KEPT ME HID?

I HAD TO FIX IT SO *NOBODY* WOULDN'T THINK OF FOLLOWING ME.

I'M EVER SO GLAD TO SEE YOU!

I AIN'T AFRAID OF *YOU* TELLING THE PEOPLE WHERE I AM.

MUSTA BEEN LONESOME...

I COULDA ATE A HOSS!

HOW DO YOU COME TO BE HERE, JIM, AND HOW'D YOU GET HERE?

...

BLAMED IF I WOULD, JIM.

WELL, I B'LIEVE YOU, HUCK.

MAYBE I BETTER NOT TELL.

WHY, JIM?

WELL, DEY'S REASONS. BUT YOU WOULDN'T TELL ON ME EF I UZ TO TELL YOU, WOULD YOU, HUCK?

JIM!

I - I RUN OFF.

WELL, I DID. I SAID I WOULDN'T, AND I'LL STICK TO IT. HONEST *INJUN*, I WILL.

PEOPLE WOULD CALL ME A LOW-DOWN ABOLITIONIST AND DESPISE ME FOR KEEPING MUM - BUT THAT DON'T MAKE NO DIFFERENCE. I AIN'T A-GOING TO TELL, AND I AIN'T A-GOING BACK THERE, ANYWAYS.

BUT MIND, YOU SAID YOU WOULDN'T TELL - YOU KNOW YOU SAID YOU WOULDN'T TELL, HUCK.

SO, NOW, LE'S KNOW ALL ABOUT IT.

OLE MISSUS - DAT'S MISS WATSON - SHE PECKS ON ME ALL DE TIME, EN TREATS ME POOTY ROUGH,

BUT SHE AWLUZ SAID SHE WOULDN'T SELL ME DOWN TO ORLEANS. BUT I NOTICED DEY WUZ A NIGGER TRADER ROUN' DE PLACE CONSIDABLE LATELY, EN I BEGIN TO GIT ONEASY.

SO YOU RAN AWAY?

DAT AIN'T ALL!

ONE NIGHT I CREEPS TO DE DO' POOTY LATE, EN I HEAR OLD MISSUS TELL DE WIDDER SHE GWYNE TO SELL ME DOWN TO ORLEANS,

I NEVER WAITED TO HEAR DE RES'. I LIT OUT MIGHTY QUICK.

BUT SHE DIDN'T WANT TO, BUT SHE COULD GIT EIGHT HUND'D DOLLARS FOR ME, EN IT 'UZ SICH A BIG STACK O'MONEY SHE COULDN'T RESIS'.

I 'SPECT'D TO STEAL A SKIFT 'LONG DE SHO' SOM'ERS 'BOVE DE TOWN, BUT DEY WUZ PEOPLE A-STIRRING YIT,

SO I HID IN DE OLE TUMBLE-DOWN COOPER-SHOP ON DE BANK TO WAIT FOR EVERYBODY TO GO 'WAY.

OH.

DAT'S WHEN I GOT TO KNOW ALL 'BOUT DE KILLIN' - I 'UZ POWERFUL SORRY YOU'S KILLED, HUCK.

BUT, I AIN'T NO MO' NOW.

CRACK

WE LAZIED ALL THAT NIGHT AFTER SUPPER –
JIM KNOWED ALL SORTS OF SIGNS AND MAGIC
THAT I HADN'T HEARD, AND HE TOLD ON 'EM.

I WARN'T
LONESOME
NO MORE.

CHAPTER IX

THE NEXT NIGHT

SSS

SSS

JIM, THIS IS NICE!

I WOULDN'T WANT TO BE NOWHERE ELSE BUT HERE.

WELL, YOU WOULDN'T A BEN HERE 'F IT HADN'T A BEN FOR JIM. YOU'D A BEN DOWN DAH IN DE WOODS WIDOUT ANY DINNER, EN GITTN' MOS' DROWNDED, TOO; DAT YOU WOULD, HONEY.

CHICKENS KNOWS WHEN IT'S GWYNE TO RAIN, EN SO DO DE BIRDS, CHILE.

I DIDN'T WANT TO MOVE TO THE CAVE AND BE CLIMBING UP AND DOWN ALL THE TIME, BUT JIM SAW SIGNS OF RAIN IN THE FLIGHT OF SOME BIRDS, AND SAID DID I WANT THE THINGS TO GET WET?

THAT'S SO.

ANYWAY, WE SET UP IN THE CAVE, AND AND DIRECTLY IT BEGUN TO RAIN, SO THE BIRDS WAS RIGHT ABOUT IT.

THE RAIN WENT ON FOR TEN OR TWELVE DAYS, UNTIL THE RIVER WAS OVER THE BANKS.

ALL THANKS TO JIM!

ONE NIGHT WE CATCHED A LITTLE SECTION OF A LUMBER RAFT – NICE PINE PLANKS.

DAYTIMES WE PADDLED ALL OVER THE ISLAND IN THE CANOE.

ANOTHER NIGHT

WE WAS UP AT THE HEAD OF THE ISLAND AND HERE COMES A FRAME-HOUSE DOWN THE RIVER.

SHE WAS A TWO-STORY, TILTED OVER CONSIDERABLE — WE SET IN THE CANOE TO WAIT FOR DAYLIGHT, THEN CLUMB IN.

HELLO, YOU!

HELLO!

ASLEEP?

ANYONE IN THERE STILL?

THERE WAS SOMETHING LAYING ON THE FLOOR THAT LOOKED LIKE A MAN.

SUH?

YOU HOLD STILL - I'LL GO EN SEE.

DAT MAN...

HIM - HOW COME?

!

IT'S A DEAD MAN. YES, INDEEDY; NAKED, TOO. HE'S BEN SHOT IN DE BACK.

WHAT IS IT?

BUT DOAN' LOOK AT HIS FACE - IT'S TOO GASHLY.

COME IN, HUCK...

SHUF

THE WAY THINGS WAS SCATTERED ABOUT WE RECKONED THE PEOPLE LEFT IN A HURRY, SO WE MADE A GOOD HAUL.

I AIN'T INTERESTED IN HIM.

WE PUT THE LOT IN THE CANOE - DIDN'T SEE NOBODY ON THE WAY BACK, AND GOT HOME ALL SAFE.

HOW'D THAT MAN COME TO BE KILLED, DO YOU RECKON?

CHAPTER X

SHOT IN THE BACK LIKE THAT?

A MAN THAT WARN'T BURIED'S MORE LIKELY TO GO A-HA'NTING AROUND THAN ONE THAT'S PLANTED AND COMFORTABLE.

SOUNDS REASONABLE.

SHUSH 'BOUT IT NOW – IT'LL BRING BAD LUCK!

BUT I COULDN'T KEEP FROM STUDYING OVER IT AND WISHING I KNOWED WHO SHOT THE MAN, AND WHAT THEY DONE IT FOR.

ANYWAY WE FOUND EIGHT DOLLARS IN SILVER SEWED UP IN THE LINING OF A COAT – THAT'S GOOD LUCK, AIN'T IT?

TWO DAYS AGO I FETCHED IN THE SNAKE-SKIN AND YOU SAID IT WAS THE WORST BAD LUCK IN THE WORLD TO TOUCH A SNAKE-SKIN WITH MY HANDS.

SHUSH NOW!

I RECKON THE PEOPLE IN THE HOUSE STOLE DAT COAT AND DI'N'T KNOW 'BOUT DE MONEY HID IN IT.

WELL, HERE'S YOUR BAD LUCK!

AND SO IT'S THEM WHO KILLED HIM?

73

DON'T YOU GIT TOO PEART. IT'S A-COMIN'.

WE'VE RAKED IN ALL THIS TRUCK AND EIGHT DOLLARS BESIDES.

I WISH WE COULD HAVE SOME BAD LUCK LIKE THIS EVERY DAY, JIM.

MIND I TELL YOU, IT'S A-COMIN'.

IT DID COME, TOO.

A FEW DAYS LATER

EH?

A SNAKE?

BIG OLD RATTLESNAKE...

HA!

BEST KILL HIM...

CRACK

THAT NIGHT

HA!

AUGH –

?

RATTLE RATTLE

UGH...

THE SNAKE'S MATE!

SSSS

SSSS

THAT ALL COMES OF MY BEING SUCH A FOOL AS TO NOT REMEMBER THAT WHEREVER YOU LEAVE A DEAD SNAKE ITS MATE ALWAYS COMES THERE AND CURLS AROUND IT.

WELL, BY NIGHT I'D FORGOT ALL ABOUT THE SNAKE, AND WHEN JIM FLUNG HIMSELF DOWN ON THE BLANKET THE SNAKE'S MATE WAS THERE, AND BIT HIM.

I'D PUT THE DEAD SNAKE ON JIM'S BLANKET, THINKIN' THERE'D BE SOME FUN WHEN JIM FOUND HIM THERE.

BAP!

BAP!

JIM! IS YOU ALL RIGHT?

JIM TOLD ME TO SKIN THE BODY AND ROAST A PIECE OF IT. I DONE IT, AND HE EAT IT, AND SAID IT WOULD HELP CURE HIM.

THEN I SLID OUT QUIET AND THREW THE SNAKES CLEAR AWAY AMONGST THE BUSHES,

FOR I WARN'T GOING TO LET JIM FIND OUT IT WAS ALL MY FAULT.

NOT IF I COULD HELP IT.

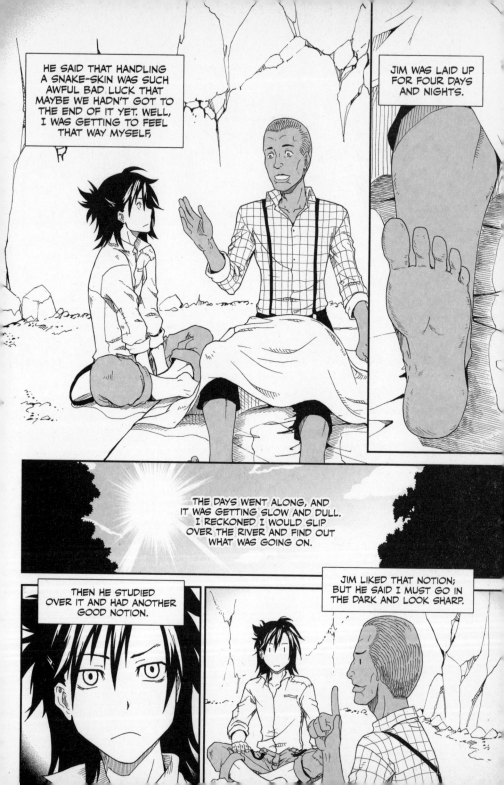

HE SAID THAT HANDLING A SNAKE-SKIN WAS SUCH AWFUL BAD LUCK THAT MAYBE WE HADN'T GOT TO THE END OF IT YET. WELL, I WAS GETTING TO FEEL THAT WAY MYSELF,

JIM WAS LAID UP FOR FOUR DAYS AND NIGHTS.

THE DAYS WENT ALONG, AND IT WAS GETTING SLOW AND DULL. I RECKONED I WOULD SLIP OVER THE RIVER AND FIND OUT WHAT WAS GOING ON.

THEN HE STUDIED OVER IT AND HAD ANOTHER GOOD NOTION.

JIM LIKED THAT NOTION; BUT HE SAID I MUST GO IN THE DARK AND LOOK SHARP.

A TOWN ON THE ILLINOIS SHORE

I AM A GIRL...
I AM A GIRL...

ALTHOUGH I PRACTICED AROUND ALL DAY, I DIDN'T MUCH WALK LIKE A GIRL.

OH! I SHOULDN'T HITCH UP MY GOWN TO GET AT MY BRITCHES-POCKET.

THIS LITTLE SHANTY AIN'T BEEN LIVED IN FOR A LONG TIME, AND NOW THERE'S A LIGHT IN THE WINDOW.

I WONDER WHO'S TAKEN UP QUARTERS THERE?

EH? I DON'T KNOW HER FACE – SHE MUST BE A STRANGER.

I WON'T FORGET! I'M A GIRL!

THAT'S GOOD. SHE WON'T KNOW MY VOICE.

CHAPTER XI

...

COME IN.

IT'S LATE – YOU MUST BE TIRED, I RECKON.

I'M MRS. JUDITH LOFTUS. WHAT MIGHT YOUR NAME BE?

WHERE 'BOUTS DO YOU LIVE? IN THIS NEIGHBORHOOD?

NO'M. IN HOOKERVILLE, SEVEN MILE BELOW. I'VE WALKED ALL THE WAY AND I'M ALL TIRED OUT.

SARAH WILLIAMS.

SHIVER

!

I SEE.

DON'T JUST STAND THERE, NOW, LET'S GO IN AND TAKE A CHEER.

ARE YOU HUNGRY? I'LL FIND YOU SOMETHING -

AH, YES...

NO'M, I AIN'T HUNGRY.

GRAB!

WHAT BRINGS YOU OUT SO LATE?

MY MOTHER'S DOWN SICK, AND OUT OF MONEY AND EVERYTHING, AND I COME TO TELL MY UNCLE ABNER MOORE.

HE LIVES AT THE UPPER END OF THE TOWN, SHE SAYS. I HAIN'T EVER BEEN HERE BEFORE. DO YOU KNOW HIM?

NO; BUT I DON'T KNOW EVERYBODY YET. I HAVEN'T LIVED HERE QUITE TWO WEEKS.

IT'S A CONSIDERABLE WAYS TO THE UPPER END OF THE TOWN. YOU BETTER STAY HERE ALL NIGHT. TAKE OFF YOUR BONNET.

NOT BY YOURSELF, YOU WON'T.

MY HUSBAND WILL BE IN BY AND BY. I'LL SEND HIM ALONG WITH YOU.

NO, I'LL REST A WHILE, I RECKON, AND GO ON. I AIN'T AFEARED OF THE DARK.

NO'M, YOU DON'T HAVE TO DO THAT.

COME ON, GET DOWN TO THE BIT WHERE I WAS MURDERED...

OH, I HEARD ABOUT THOSE GOINGS ON...

I DO AT THAT. A BOY JUST YOUR AGE NAMED HUCKLEBERRY FINN GOT HIMSELF KILLED THE OTHER DAY – I CAN'T LET YOU GO BY YOURSELF!

MOST EVERYBODY THOUGHT IT AT FIRST.

WHO DONE IT?

HE WAS SO YOUNG BUT AWFUL RICH – TEN THOUSAND DOLLARS TO HIS NAME, I HEARD.

SOME THINK OLD FINN DONE IT HIMSELF.

NO – IS THAT SO?

BUT BEFORE NIGHT THEY CHANGED AROUND AND JUDGED IT WAS DONE BY A RUNAWAY NIGGER NAMED JIM.

!!!

THE NIGGER RUN OFF THE VERY NIGHT HUCK FINN WAS KILLED.

SO THE NEXT DAY HERE COMES OLD FINN, AND HE GOES BOO-HOOING TO JUDGE THATCHER TO GET MONEY TO HUNT FOR THE NIGGER ALL OVER ILLINOIS WITH.

THE JUDGE GAVE HIM SOME, AND THAT EVENING HE GOT DRUNK, AND WAS AROUND TILL AFTER MIDNIGHT WITH A COUPLE OF MIGHTY HARD-LOOKING STRANGERS, AND THEN WENT OFF WITH THEM.

IF HE DON'T COME BACK FOR A YEAR HE'LL BE ALL RIGHT. YOU CAN'T PROVE ANYTHING ON HIM, YOU KNOW.

PEOPLE THINKS NOW THAT *HE* KILLED HIS BOY, AND FIXED THINGS SO FOLKS WOULD THINK ROBBERS DONE IT. HE'S SLY, I RECKON.

EVERYTHING WILL BE QUIETED DOWN IN A YEAR, AND HE'LL WALK IN HUCK'S MONEY AS EASY AS NOTHING.

OH, NO, NOT EVERYBODY. A GOOD MANY THINKS HE DONE IT.

YES, I RECKON SO, 'M. I DON'T SEE NOTHING IN THE WAY OF IT. HAS EVERYBODY QUIT THINKING THE NIGGER DONE IT?

I SAW SOME SMOKE AT THE END OF JACKSON'S ISLAND A COUPLE DAYS PAST, EVEN THOUGH THEY SAY THAT HARDLY ANYBODY EVER GOES THERE. LIKE AS NOT THAT NIGGER'S HIDING OVER THERE.

HUSBAND'S GOING OVER TO SEE TO-NIGHT – HIM AND ANOTHER MAN.

BUT THEY'LL GET THE NIGGER PRETTY SOON NOW, AND MAYBE THEY CAN SCARE IT OUT OF HIM.

WHY, ARE THEY AFTER HIM YET?

WELL, YOU'RE INNOCENT, AIN'T YOU! DOES THREE HUNDRED DOLLARS LAY AROUND EVERY DAY FOR PEOPLE TO PICK UP?

BAD ENOUGH HE'S A RUNAWAY NIGGER, BUT PEOPLE THINK HE'S MURDERED ME IN THE BARGAIN! WHAT SHOULD I DO?

IF THEY GO, JIM MIGHT GET HIMSELF CAUGHT...

FIDGIT

IF I CAN'T SET STILL –

I GOT TO CALM DOWN!

...

GOT TO DO SOMETHING WITH MY HANDS.

MA'AM, CAN I BE OF HELP?

THAT'S FINE.

WHAT DID YOU SAY YOUR NAME WAS, HONEY?

M – MARY WILLIAMS.

I DIDN'T SAY MARY BEFORE, DID I?

OH NO!

...

WISH SHE'D SAY SOMETHING MORE...

HONEY, I THOUGHT YOU SAID IT WAS SARAH WHEN YOU FIRST COME IN?

OH, YES'M, I DID. SARAH MARY WILLIAMS. SOME CALLS ME SARAH, SOME CALLS ME MARY.

... COME, NOW, WHAT'S YOUR REAL NAME? BILL, OR TOM, OR BOB?

PLEASE DON'T POKE FUN AT A POOR GIRL LIKE ME, MUM. IF I'M IN THE WAY HERE, I'LL –

NO, YOU WON'T. SET DOWN AND STAY WHERE YOU ARE.

SCRAPE

88

OF COURSE NOT! YOU'VE BEEN TREATED BAD. TELL ME ALL ABOUT IT, THERE'S A GOOD BOY.

YOU WOULDN'T BE LYING TO ME, WOULD YOU?

I AIN'T GOING TO HURT YOU, AND I AIN'T GOING TO TELL ON YOU, NUTHER. YOU JUST TELL ME YOUR SECRET, AND TRUST ME. I'LL KEEP IT.

YOU'RE A RUNAWAY 'PRENTICE, THAT'S ALL. IT AIN'T ANYTHING.

... ALL RIGHT.

THE... THE LAW BOUND ME TO A MEAN OLD FARMER AFTER MY PARENTS DIED, AND HE TREATS ME SO BAD I CAN'T STAND IT NO LONGER.

HE WENT AWAY TO BE GONE FOR A COUPLE OF DAYS, SO I TOOK MY CHANCE — I STOLE SOME OF HIS DAUGHTER'S OLD CLOTHES AND CLEARED OUT.

MY UNCLE ABNER MOORE WILL TAKE CARE OF ME, I BELIEVE — THAT'S WHY I STRUCK OUT FOR GOSHEN.

GOSHEN, CHILD? GOSHEN'S TEN MILE FURTHER UP THE RIVER!

WHO TOLD YOU THIS WAS GOSHEN?

SAY...

...EH?

SHIFT

WELL, THEN, A HORSE?

THE FOR'RARD END, MUM.

WHEN A COW'S LAYING DOWN, WHICH END OF HER GETS UP FIRST?

THE HIND END, MUM.

WHAT'S YOUR REAL NAME, NOW?

WELL, I RECKON YOU *HAVE* LIVED IN THE COUNTRY, I THOUGHT MAYBE YOU WAS TRYING TO HOCUS ME AGAIN.

...GEORGE PETERS, MUM.

...

WELL, TRY TO REMEMBER IT, GEORGE. DON'T FORGET AND TELL ME IT'S ELEXANDER BEFORE YOU GO.

URK-!

I PUT YOU UP A SNACK TO EAT. YOU MIGHT WANT IT ON THE WAY.

OH?

AND, BLESS YOU, CHILD, WHEN YOU SET OUT TO THREAD A NEEDLE DON'T HOLD THE THREAD STILL AND FETCH THE NEEDLE UP TO IT; HOLD THE NEEDLE STILL AND POKE THE THREAD AT IT.

I SEE...

I SPOTTED YOU FOR A BOY WHEN YOU WAS THREADING THE NEEDLE LIKE A MAN MOST ALWAYS DOES.

AND DON'T GO ABOUT WOMEN IN THAT OLD CALICO.

YOU DO A GIRL TOLERABLE POOR, BUT YOU MIGHT FOOL MEN, MAYBE.

I'LL REMEMBER THAT, MUM.

IF YOU GET IN TROUBLE, YOU SEND WORD AND I'LL DO WHAT I CAN TO GET YOU OUT OF IT.

Y-YES. THANK YOU, MUM!

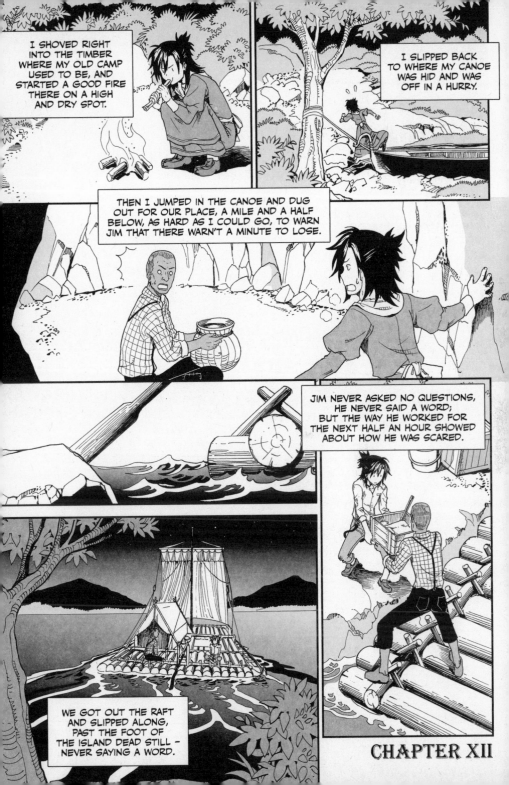

I SHOVED RIGHT INTO THE TIMBER WHERE MY OLD CAMP USED TO BE, AND STARTED A GOOD FIRE THERE ON A HIGH AND DRY SPOT.

I SLIPPED BACK TO WHERE MY CANOE WAS HID AND WAS OFF IN A HURRY.

THEN I JUMPED IN THE CANOE AND DUG OUT FOR OUR PLACE, A MILE AND A HALF BELOW, AS HARD AS I COULD GO, TO WARN JIM THAT THERE WARN'T A MINUTE TO LOSE.

JIM NEVER ASKED NO QUESTIONS, HE NEVER SAID A WORD; BUT THE WAY HE WORKED FOR THE NEXT HALF AN HOUR SHOWED ABOUT HOW HE WAS SCARED.

WE GOT OUT THE RAFT AND SLIPPED ALONG, PAST THE FOOT OF THE ISLAND DEAD STILL – NEVER SAYING A WORD.

CHAPTER XII

NEXT MORNING I FINALLY TOLD JIM ALL ABOUT THE TIME I HAD JABBERING WITH MISS LOFTUS.

WE WAS LUCKY, THOUGH, AND NOTHING EVER HAPPENED TO US ON ACCOUNT OF THAT WOMAN.

WE KEPT OURSELVES HID DURING THE DAY AND RUN AT NIGHT. EVERY NIGHT NOW I USED TO SLIP ASHORE TOWARDS TEN O'CLOCK AT SOME LITTLE VILLAGE, AND BUY MEAL OR BACON OR OTHER STUFF TO EAT.

TEN DAYS LATER

HEL-LO!

JIM, LOOKY YONDER!

THERE'S A STEAMBOAT DONE KILLED HERSELF ON A ROCK!

DOAN' LE'S GET TOO CLOS', NOW.

I DOAN' WANT TO GO FOOL'N 'LONG ER NO WRACK.

WE'S DOIN' BLAME' WELL, EN WE BETTER LET BLAME' WEL ALONE, AS DE GOOD BOOK SAYS.

LE'S LAND ON HER, JIM.

STEAMBOAT CAPTAINS IS ALWAYS RICH. I CAN'T REST TILL WE GIVE HER A RUMMAGING.

LIKE AS NOT DEY'S A WATCHMAN ON DAT WRACK.

DO YOU RECKON ANYBODY'S GOING TO RESK HIS LIFE FOR A BOAT'S LIKELY TO BREAK UP AND WASH OFF DOWN THE RIVER ANY MINUTE?

TOM SAWYER'D CALL THIS AN ADVENTURE, AND HE'D LAND ON THAT WRECK IF IT WAS HIS LAST ACT.

EF'N WE GOTS TO, LE'S TALK MIGHTY LOW, THEN.

YEAH!

...

A LIGHT...

COME ALONG, I'M FEELIN' POWERFUL SICK...

SHIVER

SHIVER

ALL RIGHT.

BY JIMMINY, SOMEONE'S HERE!

OH, PLEASE DON'T, BOYS!

I SWEAR I WON'T EVER TELL!

IT'S A LIE, JIM TURNER.

... TOM SAWYER WOULDN'T BACK OUT NOW, AND I WON'T EITHER!

YOU ALWAYS GET MORE'N YOUR SHARE OF THE TRUCK, 'CAUSE YOU'VE SWORE IF YOU DIDN'T YOU'D TELL. BUT THIS TIME YOU'VE SAID IT JEST ONE TIME TOO MANY.

I'M A-GOING TO SEE WHAT'S GOING ON HERE.

!

I'D LIKE TO PLUG YOU! AND I ORTER, TOO – A MEAN SKUNK!

BILL

OH, PLEASE DON'T, BILL; I HAIN'T EVER GOING TO TELL.

IF WE HADN'T GOT THE BEST OF YOU AND TIED YOU, YOU'D'A KILLED US BOTH!

TURNER

I DON'T WANT TO, JAKE PACKARD.

DIDN'T HE KILL OLD HATFIELD JIST THE SAME WAY – AND DON'T HE DESERVE IT?

PUT UP THAT PISTOL, BILL.

99

PACKARD

BUT I DON'T *WANT* HIM KILLED, AND I'VE GOT MY REASONS FOR IT.

BLESS YO' HEART, JAKE PACKARD! I'LL NEVER FORGIT YOU LONG'S I LIVE!

JAKE!

...!

HUH!

PAT

HERE — COME IN HERE.

ZIP

HUFF

HUFF

HE'S SAID HE'LL TELL, AND HE WILL. I'M FOR PUTTING HIM OUT OF HIS TROUBLES.

BLAME IT, I'D SORTER BEGUN TO THINK YOU WASN'T.

SHOOTING'S GOOD, BUT THERE'S QUIETER WAYS IF THE THING'S GOT TO BE DONE.

SO'M I.

MY IDEA IS THIS: WE'LL RUSTLE AROUND AND GATHER UP WHATEVER PICKINS WE'VE OVERLOOKED IN THE STATEROOMS, AND SHOVE FOR SHORE AND HIDE THE TRUCK.

THEN WE'LL WAIT. NOW I SAY IT AIN'T A-GOIN' TO BE MORE'N TWO HOURS BEFO' THIS WRACK BREAKS UP AND WASHES OFF DOWN THE RIVER. SEE? HE'LL BE DROWNDED, AND WON'T HAVE NOBODY TO BLAME FOR IT BUT HIS OWN SELF.

AIN'T I RIGHT?

YES, I RECK'N YOU ARE.

COME ALONG.

...

HUFF...

HUFF...

THUMP

A GANG SUCH AS THAT, HERE! I ALMOST GOT MURDERED FOR REAL!

I'M SORRY I COME!

...OHHH...

JIM? JIM, YOU HERE?

?

!?

RIGHT AT MY ELBOW! ... QUICK, JIM!

SHIVER

SHIVER

THERE'S A GANG OF MURDERERS IN YONDER, AND IF WE DON'T HUNT UP THEIR BOAT AND SET HER DRIFTING DOWN THE RIVER SO THESE FELLOWS CAN'T GET AWAY FROM THE WRECK THERE'S ONE OF 'EM GOING TO BE IN A BAD FIX.

BUT IF WE FIND THEIR BOAT WE CAN PUT ALL OF 'EM IN A BAD FIX - FOR THE SHERIFF'LL GET 'EM.

OH, MY LORDY, LORDY!

?

QUICK - HURRY! YOU START AT THE RAFT, AND -

CHAPTER XIII

RAF'? DEY AIN' NO RAF' NO MO'!

WHAT?

SHE DONE BROKE LOOSE EN GONE - EN HERE WE IS!

WE GOT TO FIND THEIR BOAT NOW - GOT TO HAVE IT FOR OURSELVES!

SHAKE

SHAKE

IT AIN'T NO TIME TO BE SENTIMENTERING, JIM!

SO WE WENT A-QUAKING AND SHAKING DOWN THE STABBOARD SIDE...

SEEMED A WEEK BEFORE WE GOT TO THE STERN AND FOUND THE SKIFF.

I OUT WITH MY KNIFE AND CUT THE ROPE, AND AWAY WE WENT, WITH ALL THE GANG'S PLUNDER TO BOOT!

TUMBLING AFTER ME.

SPLASH

WHEN WE WAS THREE OR FOUR HUNDRED YARDS DOWN-STREAM JIM MANNED THE OARS AND WE TOOK OUT AFTER OUR RAFT.

NOW WAS THE FIRST TIME THAT I BEGUN TO WORRY ABOUT THE MEN. I BEGUN TO THINK HOW DREADFUL IT WAS, EVEN FOR MURDERERS, TO BE IN SUCH A FIX.

AND SO, WHEN WE SAW A DOUBLE-HULL FERRYBOAT ON THE RIVER,

...

I UP AND SOBBED TO THE FERRY'S WATCHMAN A TALL STORY THAT SENT HIM TO THE WRECK SO THAT THE MURDERERS COULD BE HUNG PROPER.

SOB

SNIVEL

I WISHED THE WIDOW KNOWED ABOUT IT. I JUDGED SHE WOULD BE PROUD OF ME.

TAKE IT ALL AROUND, I WAS FEELING RUTHER COMFORTABLE ON ACCOUNTS OF TAKING ALL THIS TROUBLE FOR THAT GANG, FOR NOT MANY WOULD A DONE IT.

JIM AND I STRUCK FOR AN ISLAND TO HIDE,

AND WE SUNK THE SKIFF TOGETHER.

BY AND BY, WHEN WE GOT UP, WE TURNED OVER THE TRUCK THE GANG HAD STOLE OFF OF THE WRECK — WE HADN'T EVER BEEN THIS RICH BEFORE IN NEITHER OF OUR LIVES!

CHAPTER XIV

WE LAID OFF ALL THE AFTERNOON IN THE WOODS.

JUST TALKING, AND ME READING THE PLUNDERED BOOKS, AND HAVING A GENERAL GOOD TIME OF IT.

JIM SAID THAT HE DIDN'T WANT NO MORE ADVENTURES.

FOR IF HE DIDN'T GET SAVED HE WOULD GET DROWNDED; AND IF HE DID GET SAVED, WHOEVER SAVED HIM WOULD SEND HIM BACK HOME SO AS TO GET THE REWARD, AND THEN MISS WATSON WOULD SELL HIM SOUTH, SURE.

HE SAID THAT WHEN HE CRAWLED BACK TO GET ON THE RAFT AND FOUND HER GONE HE NEARLY DIED, BECAUSE HE JUDGED IT WAS ALL UP WITH HIM ANYWAY;

WELL, HE WAS RIGHT; HE WAS MOST ALWAYS RIGHT;

HE HAD AN UNCOMMON LEVEL HEAD FOR A NIGGER.

I DIDN'T KNOW DEY WAS SO MANY UN UM.

I HAIN'T HEARN 'BOUT NONE UN UM, SKASELY, BUT OLE KING SOLLERMUN.

?

EN WHAT DEY GOT TO DO, HUCK?

I READ CONSIDERABLE TO JIM FROM THE BOOKS, ABOUT KINGS AND DUKES AND EARLS AND SUCH.

OF COURSE IT IS. THEY JUST SET AROUND - EXCEPT, MAYBE, WHEN THERE'S A WAR; THEN THEY GO TO THE WAR. BUT OTHER TIMES THEY JUST LAZY AROUND THE HAREM.

WHAT'S DE HAREM?

NO; IS DAT SO?

THEY DON'T DO NOTHING! WHY, HOW YOU TALK!

WHY, YES, DAT'S SO.

THE PLACE WHERE THEY KEEPS THEIR WIVES. SOLOMON HAD ONE; HE HAD ABOUT A MILLION WIVES!

HE WAS THE WISEST MAN, ANYWAY - THE WIDOW SHE TOLD ME SO, HER OWN SELF.

AN' YIT DEY SAY SOLLERMUN DE WISES' MAN DAT EVER LIVE'. I DOAN' TAKE NO STOCK IN DAT.

I DOAN K'YER WHAT DE WIDDER SAY.

DOES YOU KNOW 'BOUT DAT CHILE DAT HE 'UZ GWYNE TO CHOP IN TWO?

WARN' DAT DE BEATENES' NOTION IN DE WORL'?

LE'S SAY I'S SOLLERMUN.

DOES I SHIN AROUN' MONGS' DE NEIGHBORS EN FINE OUT WHICH UN YOU DE CHILE DO B'LONG TO, EN HAN' IT OVER TO DE RIGHT ONE, ALL SAFE EN SOUN',

DE WAY DAT ANYBODY DAT HAD ANY GUMPTION WOULD?

NAW! HE 'UZ GWYNE TO CHOP DAT CHILE IN TWO!

I TAKE EN WHACK DE BILL IN *TWO*, EN GIVE HALF UN IT TO YOU, EN DE YUTHER HALF TO DE YUTHER WOMAN.

LE'S SAY DISH YER DOLLAR BILL'S DE CHILE.

WHAT'S DE USE ER DAT HALF A BILL? – CAN'T BUY NOTH'N WID IT.

EN WHAT USE IS A HALF A CHILE?

BLAME DE POINT!

BUT HANG IT, JIM, YOU'VE CLEAN MISSED THE POINT!

DOAN' TALK TO ME 'BOUT YO' PINTS.

I RECK'N I KNOWS WHAT I KNOWS. EN MINE YOU, DE *REAL* PINT IS DOWN FURDER – IT'S DOWN DEEPER.

BUT I TELL YOU YOU DON'T GET THE POINT!

I RECK'N I KNOWS SENSE WHEN I SEES IT; EN DEY AIN' NO SENSE IN SICH DOIN'S AS DAT. DE 'SPUTE WARN'T 'BOUT A HALF A CHILE, DE 'SPUTE WAS 'BOUT A WHOLE CHILE!

BUT YOU TAKE A MAN DAT'S GOT 'BOUT FIVE MILLION CHILLEN RUNNIN' ROUN' DE HOUSE, EN IT'S DIFFUNT. HE AS SOON CHOP A CHILE IN TWO AS A CAT. DEY'S PLENTY MO'. A CHILE ER TWO, MO' ER LESS, WARN'T NO CONSEKENS TO SOLLERMUN.

IT LAYS IN DE WAY SOLLERMUN WAS RAISED.

YOU TAKE A MAN DAT'S GOT ON'Y ONE OR TWO CHILLEN; IS DAT MAN GWYNE TO BE WASEFUL O' CHILLEN? NO, HE AIN'T; HE CAN'T 'FORD IT.

X 5,000,000

X 1

DAD FETCH HIM!

I NEVER SEE SUCH A NIGGER.

STILL, IT WAS NICE TO LAY OFF COMFORTABLE FOR A WHILE.

IF HE GOT A NOTION IN HIS HEAD ONCE, THERE WARN'T NO GETTING IT OUT AGAIN.

WE JUDGED THAT THREE NIGHTS MORE WOULD FETCH US TO CAIRO, AT THE BOTTOM OF ILLINOIS, WHERE THE OHIO RIVER COMES IN.

CHAPTER XV

CRUNCH
CRUNCH

WE WOULD SELL THE RAFT AND GET ON A STEAMBOAT AND GO WAY UP THE OHIO AMONGST THE FREE STATES, AND THEN BE OUT OF TROUBLE.

WELL, THE SECOND NIGHT A FOG BEGUN TO COME ON, SO WE WENT TO TIE UP THE RAFT.

I PADDLED AHEAD IN THE CANOE, BUT THERE WARN'T ANYTHING BUT LITTLE SAPLINGS TO TIE TO.

LET'S TRY THIS ONE.

SHUF

CREEEAK

!!

CRACK!

COME ON BACK AFORE THE FOG SETS IN!

I KNOW!

HUCK, WHAT YOU SAY?

!?

THE RAFT DONE BROKE THE SAPLING!

HUCK, KIN YOU HEAR ME?

JES' COME ON BACK, QUICK AS YOU CAN!

JIM, KEEP WHOOPING LOUD SO'S I CAN HEAD FOR IT!

HU-UCK-!

JIM! JIM! CAN YOU HEAR ME?

OH NO! I HAVEN'T GOT NO MORE IDEA WHICH WAY I'M GOING THAN A DEAD MAN...

IF YOU THINK IT AIN'T DISMAL AND LONESOME OUT IN A FOG THAT WAY BY YOURSELF, YOU TRY IT ONCE - YOU'LL SEE.

HEY!

HEY!

I JUST ABOUT GIVE UP THEN.

I WAS FLOATING ALONG AND OCCASIONALLY I WHOOPS, BUT I COULDN'T HEAR NO SIGN OF AN ANSWERING WHOOP NOWHERES.

I WAS GOOD AND TIRED, SO I LAID DOWN IN THE CANOE.

I DIDN'T WANT TO GO TO SLEEP, OF COURSE; BUT I WAS SO SLEEPY I COULDN'T HELP IT; SO I THOUGHT I WOULD TAKE JEST ONE LITTLE CAT-NAP.

1

BUT I RECKON IT WAS MORE THAN A CAT-NAP, FOR WHEN I WAKED UP THE STARS WAS SHINING BRIGHT, THE FOG WAS ALL GONE, AND I WAS SPINNING DOWN A BIG BEND STERN FIRST.

I LOOKED AWAY DOWN-STREAM, AND SEEN A BLACK SPECK ON THE WATER. I TOOK AFTER IT.

?

IT WAS THE RAFT.

JIM WAS SETTING THERE WITH HIS HEAD DOWN BETWEEN HIS KNEES, ASLEEP, WITH HIS RIGHT ARM HANGING OVER THE STEERING-OAR.

THE RAFT WAS LITTERED UP WITH LEAVES AND BRANCHES AND DIRT...

SO SHE'D HAD A ROUGH TIME.

HEH HEH...

GOODNESS GRACIOUS, IS DAT YOU, HUCK?

HELLO, JIM, HAVE I BEEN ASLEEP?

WHY DIDN'T YOU STIR ME UP?

DIDN'T YOU TOTE OUT DE LINE IN DE CANOE FER TO MAKE FAS' TO DE TOW-HEAD?

AND DIDN'T DE LINE PULL LOOSE EN DE RAF' GO A-HUMMIN' DOWN DE RIVER, EN LEAVE YOU EN DE CANOE BEHINE IN DE FOG?

EN YOU AIN' DEAD? IT'S TOO GOOD FER TRUE, HONEY!

WHAT'S THE MATTER WITH YOU, JIM? WHAT MAKES YOU TALK SO WILD?

WOBBLE

WOBBLE

WHY, DE FOG! - DE FOG DAT'S BEEN AROUN' ALL NIGHT. EN DIDN'T YOU WHOOP, EN DIDN'T I WHOOP, TELL WE GOT MIX' UP IN DE ISLANDS EN ONE UN US GOT LOS' EN T'OTHER ONE WAS JIS' AS GOOD AS LOS', 'KASE HE DIDN' KNOW WHAH HE WUZ?

WHAT FOG?

WELL, THIS IS TOO MANY FOR ME, JIM! OF COURSE YOU'VE BEEN DREAMING.

BUT DOG MY CATS EF IT AIN'T DE POWERFULLES DREAM I EVER SEE.

EN I HAIN'T EVER HAD NO DREAM B'FO' DAT'S TIRED ME LIKE DIS ONE!

BUT, HUCK, IT'S ALL JIS' AS PLAIN TO ME AS -

...

OH, WELL, THAT'S ALL RIGHT, BECAUSE A DREAM DOES TIRE A BODY LIKE EVERYTHING SOMETIMES.

WELL, DEN, I RECK'N I DID DREAM IT, HUCK...

IT DON'T MAKE NO DIFFERENCE HOW PLAIN IT IS; THERE AIN'T NOTHING IN IT. I KNOW, BECAUSE I'VE BEEN HERE ALL THE TIME.

120

I GOTS TO START IN AN' 'TERPRET IT.

OH, WELL, WHAT DOES *THESE* THINGS STAND FOR?

!

IT WUZ SENT FO' A MEANING. LE'S SEE. DE FIRS' TOWHEAD DONE STOOD FO' A MAN WHO GONNA TRY FER TO DO US SUM GOOD –

WHEN I GOT ALL WORE OUT WID WORK, EN WID DE CALLIN' FOR YOU, EN WENT TO SLEEP, MY HEART WUZ MOS' BROKE BEKASE YOU WUZ LOS', EN I DIDN' K'YER NO' MO' WHAT BECOME ER ME EN DE RAF'.

WHAT DO DEY STAN' FOR? I'SE GWYNE TO TELL YOU.

EN ALL YOU WUZ THINKIN' 'BOUT WUZ HOW YOU COULD MAKE A FOOL UV OLE JIM WID A LIE!

EN WHEN I WAKE UP EN FINE YOU BACK AGIN, ALL SAFE EN SOUN', DE TEARS COME, EN I COULD A GOT DOWN ON MY KNEES EN KISS YO' FOOT, I'S SO THANKFUL.

IT MADE ME FEEL SO MEAN I COULD ALMOST KISSED *HIS* FOOT TO GET HIM TO TAKE IT BACK.

SOB

SNIFFLE

I DIDN'T DO HIM NO MORE MEAN TRICKS, AND I WOULDN'T DONE THAT ONE IF I'D A KNOWED IT WOULD MAKE HIM FEEL THAT WAY.

IT WAS FIFTEEN MINUTES BEFORE I COULD WORK MYSELF UP TO GO AND HUMBLE MYSELF TO A NIGGER; BUT I DONE IT, AND I WARN'T EVER SORRY FOR IT AFTERWARDS, NEITHER.

122

OHHHH

JIM SAID IT MADE HIM ALL OVER TREMBLY AND FEVERISH TO BE SO CLOSE TO FREEDOM.

WE SLEPT MOST ALL THAT DAY, AND STARTED OUT AT NIGHT, DRIFTING DOWN INTO A BIG BEND.

WELL, I CAN TELL YOU IT MADE ME ALL OVER TREMBLY AND FEVERISH, TOO, TO HEAR HIM, BECAUSE I BEGUN TO GET IT THROUGH MY HEAD THAT HE *WAS* MOST FREE – AND WHO WAS TO BLAME FOR IT? WHY, *ME*.

CHAPTER XVI

CONSCIENCE UP AND SAYS, EVERY TIME, "BUT YOU KNOWED HE WAS RUNNING FOR HIS FREEDOM, AND YOU COULD A PADDLED ASHORE AND TOLD SOMEBODY."

I TRIED TO MAKE OUT TO MYSELF THAT I WARN'T TO BLAME, BECAUSE I DIDN'T RUN JIM OFF FROM HIS RIGHTFUL OWNER; BUT IT WARN'T NO USE.

"WHY, SHE TRIED TO LEARN YOU YOUR BOOK, SHE TRIED TO LEARN YOU YOUR MANNERS, SHE TRIED TO BE GOOD TO YOU EVERY WAY SHE KNOWED HOW. *THAT'S* WHAT SHE DONE."

"WHAT HAD POOR MISS WATSON DONE TO YOU THAT YOU COULD SEE HER NIGGER GO OFF RIGHT UNDER YOUR EYES AND NEVER SAY ONE SINGLE WORD?"

I GOT TO FEELING SO MEAN AND SO MISERABLE I MOST WISHED I WAS DEAD.

JIM WAS SAYING HOW THE FIRST THING HE WOULD DO WHEN HE GOT TO A FREE STATE HE WOULD GO TO SAVING UP MONEY AND NEVER SPEND A SINGLE CENT.

AND HOW WHEN HE GOT ENOUGH HE WOULD BUY HIS WIFE, AND THEN THEY WOULD BOTH WORK TO BUY THE TWO CHILDREN –

– AND IF THEIR MASTER WOULDN'T SELL THEM, THEY'D GET AN AB'LITIONIST TO GO AND STEAL THEM!

!

THIS IS WHAT COMES OF MY NOT THINKING...

WHAT? HE WOULDN'T EVER DARE TO TALK SUCH TALK IN HIS LIFE BEFORE!

HERE'S THIS NIGGER, WHICH I'VE AS GOOD AS HELPED TO RUN AWAY, COMING RIGHT OUT FLAT-FOOTED AND SAYING HE'D STEAL HIS CHILDREN –

CHILDREN THAT BELONG TO A MAN I DON'T EVEN KNOW; A MAN THAT HAIN'T EVER DONE ME NO HARM!

WE'S SAFE, HUCK, WE'S SAFE! JUMP UP AND CRACK YO' HEELS! DAT'S DE GOOD OLE CAIRO AT LAS', I JIS KNOWS IT!

LET UP ON ME, CONSCIENCE - IT AIN'T TOO LATE YET-

I'LL PADDLE ASHORE AT THE FIRST LIGHT AND TELL.

POOTY SOON I'LL BE A-SHOUT'N' FOR JOY!

IT MIGHTN'T BE, YOU KNOW. I'LL TAKE THE CANOE AND GO AND SEE.

IT'S ALL ON ACCOUNTS O' HUCK; JIM WON'T EVER FORGIT YOU!

...

HUCK; YOU'S DE BES' FREN' JIM'S EVER HAD; EN YOU'S DE ONLY FREN' OLE JIM'S GOT NOW.

DAH YOU GOES, DE OLE TRUE HUCK; DE ON'Y WHITE GENLMAN DAT EVER KEP' HIS PROMISE TO OLE JIM.

...

WELL, I JUST FELT SICK.

BUT I SAYS, I GOT TO DO IT - I CAN'T GET OUT OF IT.

EVENIN'.

I... I GOT TO.

SPLASH

SPLASH

OH! A SKIFF...

126

YOU'RE OUT MIGHTY LATE.

YOU'D BEST BE KEEPING SAFE.

PARKER

JOHN

DO YOU BELONG ON IT?

YES, SIR.

A PIECE OF A RAFT.

WHAT'S THAT YONDER?

!

ANY MEN ON IT?

ONLY ONE, SIR.

UP YONDER, ABOVE THE HEAD OF THE BEND.

WELL, THERE'S FIVE NIGGERS RUN OFF TO-NIGHT.

IS YOUR MAN WHITE OR BLACK?

I DIDN'T ANSWER UP PROMPT. I TRIED TO, BUT THE WORDS WOULDN'T COME.

SO... I GIVE UP TRYING.

I RECKON WE'LL GO AND SEE FOR OURSELVES.

I WISH YOU WOULD.

HE'S WHITE.

MAYBE YOU'D HELP ME TOW THE RAFT ASHORE WHERE THE LIGHT IS?

IT'S PAP THAT'S THERE. HE'S SICK — AND SO IS MAM AND MARY ANN.

I S'POSE WE'VE GOT TO.

PAP'LL BE MIGHTY MUCH OBLEEGED TO YOU, I CAN TELL YOU.

...

EVERYBODY GOES AWAY WHEN I WANT THEM TO HELP ME TOW THE RAFT ASHORE, AND I CAN'T DO IT BY MYSELF.

IT'S THE — A — THE — WELL, IT AIN'T ANYTHING MUCH.

BOY, THAT'S A LIE.

WELL, THAT'S INFERNAL MEAN. ODD, TOO.

SAY, BOY, WHAT'S THE MATTER WITH YOUR FATHER?

I AIN'T LYIN'...

BOY, YOU ARE.

WHAT IS THE MATTER WITH YOUR PAP? ANSWER UP SQUARE NOW, AND IT'LL BE THE BETTER FOR YOU.

I WILL, SIR, I WILL, HONEST — BUT DON'T LEAVE US, PLEASE. IT'S THE — THE —

YOUR PAP'S GOT THE SMALL-POX, AND YOU KNOW IT PRECIOUS WELL! WHY DIDN'T YOU COME OUT AND SAY SO? DO YOU WANT TO SPREAD IT ALL OVER?

!

WAAAAH

...

SOB

SOB

WELL - WELL -

SOB

POOR DEVIL, THERE'S SOMETHING IN THAT.

I'VE TOLD EVERYBODY BEFORE, AND THEY JUST WENT AWAY AND LEFT US!

THEY WAS TOO AFRAID OF THE SMALL-POX TO COME EVEN A BIT CLOSER. THEY RECKONED WE WERE IN SOME HARD LUCK, TOO, SO THEY PUT A TWENTY-DOLLAR GOLD PIECE ON A BOARD AND FLOATED IT DOWN TO ME WHERE I WAS.

I SEE IT WARN'T NO USE FOR ME TO TRY TO LEARN TO DO RIGHT.

THEY WENT OFF AND I WAS FEELING BAD AND LOW, BECAUSE I KNOWED VERY WELL I HAD DONE WRONG.

!

JIM?

I SLIPS INTO DE RIVER EN WAS GWYNE TO SHOVE FOR SHO' IF DEY COME ABOARD.

LAWSY, HOW YOU DID FOOL 'EM, HUCK!

I TELL YOU, CHILE, I 'SPEC IT SAVE' OLE JIM – OLE JIM AIN'T GOING TO FORGIT YOU FOR DAT, HONEY.

I THOUGHT A MINUTE, AND SAYS TO MYSELF, HOLD ON; S'POSE YOU'D A DONE RIGHT AND GIVE JIM UP, WOULD YOU FELT BETTER THAN WHAT YOU DO NOW?

SPLASH

I'D FEEL JUST THE SAME WAY I DO NOW.

NO, SAYS I, I'D FEEL BAD —

WELL, THEN, SAYS I, WHAT'S THE USE YOU LEARNING TO DO RIGHT WHEN IT'S TROUBLESOME TO DO RIGHT AND AIN'T NO TROUBLE TO DO WRONG, AND THE WAGES IS JUST THE SAME?

I WAS STUCK. I COULDN'T ANSWER THAT.

SO I RECKONED I WOULDN'T BOTHER NO MORE ABOUT IT, BUT AFTER THIS ALWAYS DO WHICHEVER COME HANDIEST AT THE TIME.

WE'D BEGUN TO SUSPICION SOMETHING AFTER A BIT, THOUGH. MAYBE WE ALREADY WENT BY CAIRO - IN THE FOG THAT NIGHT...?

I WISH I'D NEVER SEEN THAT SNAKE-SKIN!

WHOOOOOOOOO -

WHAT'S MORE, WE'D SHOVED OUT AFTER DARK, AIMING TO BUY A CANOE TO GO BACK UP-STREAM, AND ALONG COMES A STEAMBOAT UP THE RIVER!

CRASH-

THERE WAS A YELL AT US, AND A JINGLING OF BELLS TO STOP THE ENGINES, A POWWOW OF CUSSING, AND WHISTLING OF STEAM - AND AS JIM WENT OVERBOARD ON ONE SIDE AND I ON THE OTHER, SHE COME SMASHING STRAIGHT THROUGH THE RAFT.

I GRABBED A PLANK THAT TOUCHED ME WHILE I WAS "TREADING WATER," AND STRUCK OUT FOR SHORE, SHOVING IT AHEAD OF ME.

HUFF

HUFF

I'D SUNG OUT FOR JIM ABOUT A DOZEN TIMES WITHOUT ANY ANSWER.

I WENT POKING ALONG OVER ROUGH GROUND FOR A QUARTER OF A MILE OR MORE.

RUSTLE

RUSTLE

AND I RUN ACROSS A BIG OLD-FASHIONED DOUBLE LOG-HOUSE BEFORE I NOTICED IT.

CHAPTER XVII

HOWWWWWWL!

RUFF!

BARK!

BE DONE, BOYS!

WHO'S THERE?

IT'S ME – AH, GEORGE JACKSON, SIR.

WHAT ARE YOU PROWLING AROUND HERE THIS TIME OF NIGHT FOR – HEY?

!

I WASN'T PROWLING AROUND, SIR. I FELL OVERBOARD OFF THE STEAMBOAT.

IF YOU'RE TELLING THE TRUTH, THEN YOU NEEDN'T BE AFRAID – NOBODY WILL HURT YOU. BUT DON'T TRY TO BUDGE; STAND RIGHT WHERE YOU ARE. IS THERE ANYBODY WITH YOU?

NO, SIR, NOBODY.

ROUSE OUT BOB AND TOM, SOME OF YOU, AND FETCH THE GUNS.

ALL READY.

NOW, GEORGE JACKSON:

WHAT'S GOING ON IN THERE?

DO YOU KNOW THE SHEPHERD-SONS?

WELL, THAT MAY BE SO, AND IT MAYN'T.

NO, SIR; I NEVER HEARD OF THEM.

STEP FORWARD, GEORGE JACKSON. AND MIND, DON'T YOU HURRY - COME MIGHTY SLOW. IF THERE'S ANYBODY WITH YOU, LET HIM KEEP BACK - IF HE SHOWS HIMSELF HE'LL BE SHOT.

PUSH THE DOOR OPEN A LITTLE BIT BY YOURSELF - JUST ENOUGH TO SQUEEZE IN, D' YOU HEAR?

COME ALONG NOW. COME SLOW.

THERE, THAT'S ENOUGH - PUT YOUR HEAD IN.

WHAT...

CREEEE

I CAN HEAR MY HEART!

THEY'RE GOING TO TAKE MY HEAD OFF IF'N I PUT IT IN.

THERE; I RECKON IT'S ALL RIGHT. COME IN.

WHY, *HE* AIN'T A SHEPHERDSON.

NO, THERE AIN'T ANY SHEPHERDSON ABOUT HIM.

TOM GRANGERFORD

COLONEL SAUL GRANGERFORD

BOB GRANGERFORD

THREE BIG MEN WITH GUNS POINTED AT ME...

WHO'S THAT BACK THERE?

SOPHIA GRANGERFORD

CHARLOTTE GRANGERFORD

RACHEL GRANGERFORD

WELL, THAT'S ALL RIGHT.

PAT PAT

I DON'T MEAN NO HARM BY IT.

I HOPE YOU WON'T MIND BEING CHECKED FOR ARMS.

I MEANT NO HARM BY IT – MAKE YOURSELF EASY AND AT HOME.

IT'S ALL RIGHT.

WHY, BLESS YOU, SAUL.

BETSY, YOU FLY AROUND AND GET HIM SOMETHING TO EAT AS QUICK AS YOU CAN, POOR THING; AND ONE OF YOU GIRLS GO AND WAKE UP BUCK AND TELL HIM –

THE POOR THING'S AS WET AS HE CAN BE; AND DON'T YOU RECKON IT MAY BE HE'S HUNGRY?

YES'M.

AIN'T THEY NO SHEPHERDSONS AROUND?

YAWWWWWWN –

OH, HERE HE IS HIMSELF.

NO, 'TWAS A FALSE ALARM.

BUCK GRANGERFORD

WELL, IF THEY'D A BEN SOME, I RECKON I'D A GOT ONE.

BUCK, TAKE THIS LITTLE STRANGER AND GET THE WET CLOTHES OFF HIM. LEND HIM SOME OF YOUR DRY CLOTHES.

HA! WHY, BUCK, THEY MIGHT HAVE SCALPED US ALL, YOU'VE BEEN SO SLOW IN COMING.

142

GO 'LONG WITH YOU NOW, AND DO AS BOB TOLD YOU.

WELL...

NEVER MIND, BUCK, MY BOY, YOU'LL HAVE SHOW ENOUGH, ALL IN GOOD TIME.

WELL, NOBODY COME AFTER ME, AND IT AIN'T RIGHT I'M ALWAYS KEPT DOWN; I DON'T GET NO SHOW.

HMPH!

COME ON AND I'LL GET YOU SOME OF MY CLOTHES.

ALL RIGHT.

YOU LOOK LIKE WE'RE OF A SIZE.

WE GOT TO TALKING AND TELLING RIDDLES, AND AFTER A BIT IT WAS ALMOST LIKE WE WERE FRIENDS. I WAS STAYING ON IN HIS ROOM, SINCE HE HAD A BED AND ALL.

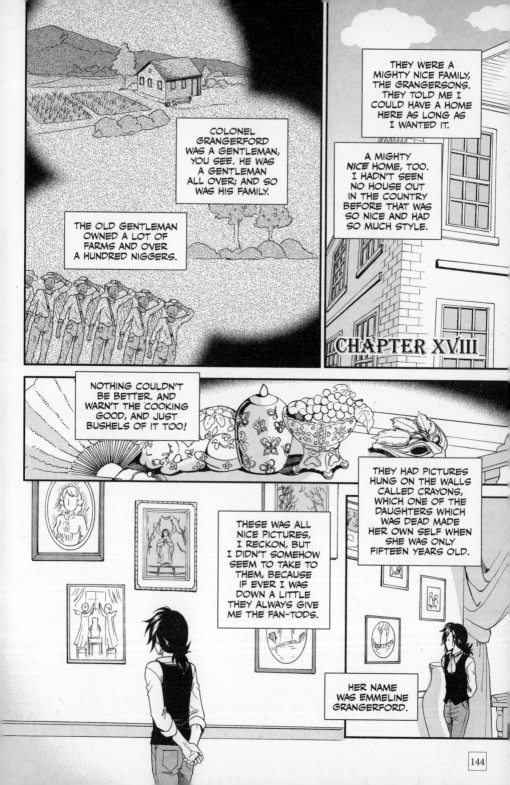

COLONEL GRANGERFORD WAS A GENTLEMAN, YOU SEE. HE WAS A GENTLEMAN ALL OVER; AND SO WAS HIS FAMILY.

THE OLD GENTLEMAN OWNED A LOT OF FARMS AND OVER A HUNDRED NIGGERS.

THEY WERE A MIGHTY NICE FAMILY, THE GRANGERSONS. THEY TOLD ME I COULD HAVE A HOME HERE AS LONG AS I WANTED IT.

A MIGHTY *NICE* HOME, TOO. I HADN'T SEEN NO HOUSE OUT IN THE COUNTRY BEFORE THAT WAS SO NICE AND HAD SO MUCH STYLE.

CHAPTER XVIII

NOTHING COULDN'T BE BETTER. AND WARN'T THE COOKING GOOD, AND JUST BUSHELS OF IT TOO!

THEY HAD PICTURES HUNG ON THE WALLS CALLED CRAYONS, WHICH ONE OF THE DAUGHTERS WHICH WAS DEAD MADE HER OWN SELF WHEN SHE WAS ONLY FIFTEEN YEARS OLD.

THESE WAS ALL NICE PICTURES, I RECKON, BUT I DIDN'T SOMEHOW SEEM TO TAKE TO THEM, BECAUSE IF EVER I WAS DOWN A LITTLE THEY ALWAYS GIVE ME THE FAN-TODS.

HER NAME WAS EMMELINE GRANGERFORD.

144

I LIKED ALL THAT FAMILY, DEAD ONES AND ALL.

THIS YOUNG GIRL KEPT A SCRAP-BOOK WHEN SHE WAS ALIVE, AND USED TO PASTE OBITUARIES AND ACCIDENTS AND CASES OF PATIENT SUFFERING IN IT OUT OF THE PRESBYTERIAN OBSERVER,

AND WRITE POETRY AFTER THEM OUT OF HER OWN HEAD. IT WAS VERY GOOD POETRY.

THEY WAS AS HIGH-TONED AND WELL BORN AND RICH AND GRAND AS THE TRIBE OF GRANGERFORDS.

THERE WAS ANOTHER CLAN OF ARISTOCRACY AROUND THERE - FIVE OR SIX FAMILIES - MOSTLY OF THE NAME OF SHEPHERDSON.

BANG BANG

PTWEE!

THE TWO FAMILIES HATED EACH OTHER LIKE POISON, THOUGH I DIDN'T KNOW JUST HOW BAD IT WAS, AT FIRST.

QUICK! JUMP FOR THE WOODS!

ONE DAY BUCK AND ME WAS AWAY OUT IN THE WOODS HUNTING, AND HEARD A HORSE COMING. IT WAS YOUNG HARNEY SHEPHERDSON.

I HEARD BUCK'S GUN GO OFF AT MY EAR, AND HARNEY'S HAT TUMBLED OFF FROM HIS HEAD.

WE STARTED THROUGH THE WOODS ON A RUN AND NEVER STOPPED RUNNING TILL WE GOT HOME.

THE OLD GENTLEMAN'S EYES BLAZED A MINUTE WHEN BUCK TOLD HIM - 'TWAS PLEASURE, MAINLY, I JUDGED - THEN HIS FACE SORT OF SMOOTHED DOWN.

AS FOR ME, I WAS CONFUSED. WHY DIDN'T HARNEY SHOOT BACK?

THE COLONEL ONLY SAID THAT HE DIDN'T LIKE BUCK SHOOTING FROM BEHIND A BUSH.

DID YOU WANT TO KILL HIM, BUCK?

WELL, I BET I DID.

WHAT DID HE DO TO YOU?

HIM? HE NEVER DONE NOTHING TO ME.

WELL, THEN, WHAT DID YOU WANT TO KILL HIM FOR?

WHY, NOTHING - ONLY IT'S ON ACCOUNT OF THE FEUD.

WHAT'S A FEUD?

NEVER HEARD OF IT BEFORE - TELL ME ABOUT IT.

WHY, WHERE WAS YOU RAISED? DON'T YOU KNOW WHAT A FEUD IS?

WELL...

A FEUD IS THIS WAY: A MAN HAS A QUARREL WITH ANOTHER MAN, AND KILLS HIM;

THEN THAT OTHER MAN'S BROTHER KILLS *HIM*;

THEN THE OTHER BROTHERS, ON BOTH SIDES, GOES FOR ONE ANOTHER; THEN THE *COUSINS* CHIP IN –

BY AND BY EVERYBODY'S BEEN KILLED OFF, AND THERE AIN'T NO MORE FEUD.

WHAT WAS THE TROUBLE ABOUT, BUCK? – LAND?

HAS IT BEEN GOING ON LONG, BUCK?

I RECKON MAYBE – I DON'T KNOW.

WELL, I SHOULD RECKON! IT STARTED THIRTY YEAR AGO, OR SOM'ERS ALONG THERE.

WELL, WHO DONE THE SHOOTING?

LAWS, HOW DO I KNOW? IT WAS SO LONG AGO.

OH, YES, PA KNOWS, I RECKON, AND SOME OF THE OTHER OLD PEOPLE.

DON'T ANYBODY KNOW?

HAS THERE BEEN MANY KILLED, BUCK?

YES; RIGHT SMART CHANCE OF FUNERALS.

'BOUT THREE MONTHS AGO MY COUSIN BUD, FOURTEEN YEAR OLD, WAS RIDING THROUGH THE WOODS ON T'OTHER SIDE OF THE RIVER...

BUD DIDN'T HAVE NO WEAPON WITH HIM, WHICH WAS BLAME' FOOLISHNESS.

HE HEARS A HORSE A-COMING BEHIND HIM, AND SEES OLD BALDY SHEPHERDSON A-LINKIN' AFTER HIM WITH HIS GUN IN HIS HAND AND HIS WHITE HAIR A-FLYING IN THE WIND.

HE SEEN IT WARN'T ANY USE, SO HE STOPPED AND FACED AROUND SO AS TO HAVE THE BULLET HOLES IN FRONT, YOU KNOW,

AND THE OLD MAN HE RODE UP AND SHOT HIM DOWN.

PAK PAK PAK PAK PAK

BUT HE DIDN'T GIT MUCH CHANCE TO ENJOY HIS LUCK, FOR INSIDE OF A WEEK OUR FOLKS LAID *HIM* OUT.

I RECKON THAT OLD MAN WAS A COWARD, BUCK.

HUFF

I RECKON HE **WARN'T** A COWARD. NOT BY A BLAME' SIGHT.

...

THERE AIN'T A COWARD AMONGST THEM SHEPHERDSONS – NOT A ONE.

WHY, THAT OLD MAN KEP' UP HIS END IN A FIGHT ONE DAY FOR HALF AN HOUR AGAINST THREE GRANGERFORDS, AND COME OUT WINNER.

BUT...

WHAT ABOUT HARNEY SHEPHERDSON?

BANG!

PAK

PAK

PAK

TWICE HE DONE COVERED BUCK WITH HIS GUN, BUT THEN HE JUST RODE AWAY THE WAY HE COME.

AND MISS SOPHIA...

WHEW...

SHE TURNED PALE AT BUCK'S STORY –

– BUT THE COLOR COME BACK WHEN SHE FOUND HARNEY WARN'T HURT.

HOW MUCH FURTHER, JACK?

YOU SHOVE RIGHT IN DAH JIST A FEW STEPS, MARS JAWGE; DAH'S WHAH DEY IS.

JACK

MIGHTY CURIOUS. HE OUGHTER KNOW A BODY DON'T LOVE WATER-MOCCASINS ENOUGH TO GO AROUND HUNTING FOR THEM.

HE TRIED TO BRING ME HERE YESTERDAY, TOO.

WHAT IS HE UP TO, ANYWAY?

THE MEN TOOK THEIR GUNS ALONG, SO DID BUCK, AND KEPT THEM BETWEEN THEIR KNEES OR STOOD THEM HANDY AGAINST THE WALL. THE SHEPHERDSONS DONE THE SAME.

THIS MORNING WE ALL WENT TO CHURCH, ABOUT THREE MILE, EVERYBODY A-HORSEBACK...

BONG BONG

BONG

IT WAS PRETTY ORNERY PREACHING – ALL ABOUT BROTHERLY LOVE, AND SUCH-LIKE TIRESOMENESS.

IT DID SEEM TO ME TO BE ONE OF THE ROUGHEST SUNDAYS I HAD RUN ACROSS YET.

EVERYBODY SAID IT WAS A GOOD SERMON, AND THEY ALL HAD SUCH A POWERFUL LOT TO SAY ABOUT FAITH AND GOOD WORKS AND FREE GRACE AND PREFOREORDESTINATION, AND I DON'T KNOW WHAT ALL.

AND THEN MISS SOPHIA ASKED ME IF I LIKED HER, AND I SAID I DID; AND SHE ASKED ME IF I WOULD DO SOMETHING FOR HER AND NOT TELL ANYBODY, AND I SAID I WOULD...

THEN SHE SAID SHE'D FORGOT HER TESTAMENT, AND LEFT IT IN THE SEAT AT CHURCH BETWEEN TWO OTHER BOOKS, AND WOULD I SLIP OUT QUIET AND GO THERE AND FETCH IT TO HER?

ANYWAY ON THE WAY BACK I GIVE IT A SHAKE, AND OUT DROPS A LITTLE PIECE OF PAPER WITH *"HALF-PAST TWO"* WROTE ON IT WITH A PENCIL.

GEORGE, YOU'RE THE BEST BOY IN THE WORLD!

BETTER NOT TELL HER I READ IT...

HER EYES LIGHTED UP, AND IT MADE HER POWERFUL PRETTY.

...

I'S SEED 'M BEFO'; I DON'T K'YER TO SEE 'EM NO MO'.

YOU SHOVE RIGHT IN DAH JIST A FEW STEPS, MARS JAWGE; DAH'S WHAH DEY IS.

MIGHT AS WELL POKE INTO THE PLACE A-WAYS.

SHUFF

BY JINGS IF IT AIN'T MY OLD JIM!

AIN'T THIS A GRAND SURPRISE?

JIM NEARLY CRIED, HE WAS SO GLAD TO SEE ME AGAIN.

JACK HE BRINGS ME TRUCK TO EAT EVERY NIGHT, EN TELLS ME HOW YOU'S A-GITT'N ALONG.

SO WHAT HAPPENED TO YOU WHEN THE RAFT GOT ALL SMASHED UP, JIM?

I GOT HURT A LITTLE, EN COULDN'T SWIM FAS', SO I WUZ A CONSIDABLE WAYS BEHINE YOU TOWARDS DE LAS'; WHEN YOU LANDED I RECK'NE I COULD KETCH UP WID YOU.

BUT WHEN I SAW DAT HOUSE I BEGIN TO GO SLOW. I 'UZ OFF TOO FUR TO HEAR WHAT DEY SAY TO YOU – I WUZ 'FRAID O' DE DOGS.

EARLY IN DE MAWNIN' SOME ER DE NIGGERS COME ALONG, GWYNE TO DE FIELDS, EN DEY TUK ME EN SHOWED ME DIS PLACE, WHAH DE DOGS CAN'T TRACK ME ON ACCOUNTS O' DE WATER.

WHY DIDN'T YOU TELL MY JACK TO FETCH ME HERE SOONER, JIM?

WELL, 'TWARN'T NO USE TO 'STURB YOU, HUCK, TELL WE COULD DO SUMFN.

I BEN A-BUYIN' POTS EN PANS EN VITTLES, AS I GOT A CHANST, EN A-PATCHIN' UP DE RAF' NIGHTS WHEN –

NO, SHE WARN'T. SHE WAS TORE UP A GOOD DEAL - ONE EN' OF HER WAS; BUT DEY WARN'T NO GREAT HARM DONE, ON'Y OUR TRAPS WAS MOS' ALL LOS'.

YOU MEAN TO SAY OUR OLD RAFT WARN'T SMASHED ALL TO FLINDERS?

NOW SHE'S ALL FIXED UP AGIN MOS' AS GOOD AS NEW, EN WE'S GOT A NEW LOT O' STUFF, IN DE PLACE O' WHAT UZ LOS'.

WE'S ALL RIGHT NOW!

ALL RIGHT.

I DON'T WANT TO TALK MUCH ABOUT THE NEXT DAY.

I RECKON I'LL CUT IT PRETTY SHORT.

EVERYTHING'S AS STILL AS A MOUSE...

MISS SOPHIA'S RUN OFF - TO GET MARRIED TO DAT YOUNG HARNEY SHEPHERDSON, YOU KNOW!

WHAT'S IT ALL ABOUT, JACK?

DON'T YOU KNOW, MARS JAWGE?

WHAT?!

BUCK WENT OFF 'THOUT WAKING ME UP.

WELL, I RECK'N HE DID!

DEY WARN'T GWYNE TO MIX YOU UP IN IT.

DE WOMEN FOLKS HAS GONE FOR TO STIR UP DE RELATIONS, EN OLE MARS SAUL EN DE BOYS TUCK DEY GUNS EN RODE UP DE RIVER ROAD FOR TO TRY TO KETCH DAT YOUNG MAN EN KILL HIM 'FO' HE KIN GIT ACROST DE RIVER WID MISS SOPHIA.

...

MARS BUCK HE LOADED UP HIS GUN EN 'LOWED HE'S GWYNE TO FETCH HOME A SHEPHERDSON OR BUST.

BUCK!

LAWS BLESS YOU, MARS JAWGE, TAKE CARE!

HUFF... HUFF...

SLAM

GOT TO GET TO THE STEAMBOAT LANDING...

BANG! BANG!

BANG!

GUNS, A GOOD WAYS OFF!

NEED TO FIND A PLACE TO HIDE BEFORE I GET SHOT AT...

THUMP

I CAN SEE THE LOG STORE FROM HERE.

SHEPHERDSONS ON THEIR HORSES...

!

THAT'S BUCK!

BUCK, UP HERE!

!

THEY'RE RUNNING THIS WAY WHILE THE SHEPHERDSONS ARE DISTRACTED...

THEY'S OUT OF SIGHT NOW, BUCK. LET'S GO BACK TO THE HOUSE!

GEORGE? WHY ARE YOU HERE?

FATHER OUGHT TO HAVE WAITED FOR OUR RELATIONS – THE SHEPHERDSONS WERE TOO STRONG FOR THEM ALONE!

SNF

NO! THEY'S JUST UP TO SOME DEVILMENT OR OTHER – THEY LAID FOR US IN AMBUSH! MY FATHER AND BROTHERS WAS KILLED ALREADY!

WHAT ?!

WHAT... WHAT'S BECOME OF HARNEY AND MISS SOPHIA?

HAH! THEY GOT ACROSS THE RIVER. THEY'S PROBABLY SAFE.

I'M GLAD OF THAT...

WE GOT TWO OR THREE OF THEM, AT ANY RATE...

RIGHT.

BUCK, LET'S GO.

IF I'D ONLY MANAGED TO KILL HARNEY SHEPHERDSON THAT DAY – FATHER... TOM... BOB... !

GEORGE, GO ON BACK UP TO THE HOUSE WHEN YOU CAN.

YOU AIN'T NO GRANGERFORD, SO YOU AIN'T NO PART OF THIS.

WHAT ABOUT YOU?

GRANGERFORDS! KILL THEM! KILL THEM!

JOE AND I... WE'LL MAKE UP FOR THIS DAY YET!

I STAYED IN THE TREE TILL IT BEGUN TO GET DARK, AFRAID TO COME DOWN.

SOMETIMES I HEARD GUNS AWAY OFF IN THE WOODS; AND TWICE I SEEN LITTLE GANGS OF MEN GALLOP PAST THE LOG STORE WITH GUNS.

IT'S THE YOUNGEST - KILL HIM!

BANG!

BANG!

BANG!

BANG!

WHEN I GOT DOWN OUT OF THE TREE I CREPT ALONG DOWN THE RIVER BANK A PIECE.

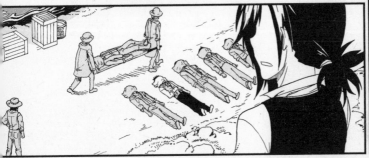

I MADE UP MY MIND I WOULDN'T EVER GO ANEAR THAT HOUSE AGAIN.

HUFF HUFF HUFF

SHUFF

I RECKON I'M TO BLAME!

I JUDGED I OUGHT TO TOLD MISS SOPHIA'S FATHER ABOUT THAT PAPER AND THE CURIOUS WAY SHE ACTED, AND THEN MAYBE HE WOULD A LOCKED HER UP, AND THIS AWFUL MESS WOULDN'T EVER HAPPENED.

HE WAS MIGHTY GOOD TO ME!

THAT WAS BUCK, KILT, WITH HIS FACE ALL COVERED UP...

I WAS MIGHTY DOWNHEARTED.

I WISHED I HADN'T EVER COME ASHORE THAT NIGHT TO SEE SUCH THINGS.

I AIN'T A-GOING TO TELL ALL THAT HAPPENED - IT WOULD MAKE ME SICK AGAIN IF I WAS TO DO THAT.

I AIN'T EVER GOING TO GET SHUT OF THEM - LOTS OF TIMES I DREAM ABOUT THEM.

WHUMP

SIIIIGH

I NEVER FELT EASY TILL THE RAFT WAS TWO MILE BELOW THERE AND OUT IN THE MIDDLE OF THE MISSISSIPPI.

I WAS POWERFUL GLAD TO GET AWAY FROM THE FEUDS, AND SO WAS JIM TO GET AWAY FROM THE SWAMP.

WE RUN NIGHTS, AND LAID UP AND HID DAYTIMES.

CHAPTER XIX

WE'D TAKE SOME FISH OFF OF THE LINES AND COOK UP A HOT BREAKFAST,

AND AFTERWARDS WE WOULD WATCH THE LONESOMENESS OF THE RIVER, AND KIND OF LAZY ALONG, AND BY AND BY LAZY OFF TO SLEEP.

TWO OR THREE DAYS AND NIGHTS WENT BY; I RECKON I MIGHT SAY THEY SWUM BY, THEY SLID ALONG SO QUIET AND SMOOTH AND LOVELY.

ONE MORNING ABOUT DAYBREAK I PADDLED ABOUT A MILE UP A CRICK AMONGST THE CYPRESS WOODS, TO SEE IF I COULDN'T GET SOME BERRIES.

!?

STEP STEP STEP STEP

FOOTSTEPS – MIGHT BE SOMEBODY AFTER ME? OR AFTER JIM?

WAIT, THAT CAN'T BE...

I ONLY JUST FOUND THIS CANOE AND LANDED – HOW'D ANYONE KNOW I WAS HERE?

!

HELP!

I'M BEGGING YOU, SAVE OUR LIVES!

GASP

WHEEZE

HUFF

HUFF

HUFF

WE HAVEN'T BEEN DOING NOTHING, AND WE'RE BEING CHASED FOR IT! THERE'S MEN AND DOGS A-COMING!

HOLD ON!

TAKE TO THE WATER AND WADE DOWN TO ME AND GET IN - THAT'LL THROW THE DOGS OFF THE SCENT.

SPLASH

SPLASH

ALL RIGHT!

PHEW!

RECKON WE'RE SAFE NOW?

THEY DONE IT, AND I LIT OUT FOR OUR TOWHEAD.

WHAT GOT YOU INTO TROUBLE?

WELL, I'D BEEN SELLING AN ARTICLE TO TAKE THE TARTAR OFF THE TEETH.

RECK'N IT'S SAFE NOW.

THOUGHT I WAS DEAD THIS TIME FOR SURE...

WHEW

HUFF

HUFF HUFF

IT DOES TAKE IT OFF, TOO, AND GENERLY THE ENAMEL ALONG WITH IT.

...

AND WAS JUST IN THE ACT OF SLIDING OUT WHEN I RAN ACROSS YOU ON THE TRAIL THIS SIDE OF TOWN.

I STAYED ABOUT ONE NIGHT LONGER THAN I OUGHT TO,

SO I TOLD YOU I WAS EXPECTING TROUBLE MYSELF, AND WOULD SCATTER OUT WITH YOU.

ANYWAY, YOU TOLD ME THEY WERE COMING, AND BEGGED ME TO HELP YOU TO GET OFF.

SO THESE CHAPS DON'T KNOW ONE ANOTHER...

WELL, I'D BEN A-RUNNIN' A LITTLE TEMPERANCE REVIVAL THAR 'BOUT A WEEK.

THAT'S THE WHOLE YARN — WHAT'S YOURN?

I WAS TAKIN' AS MUCH AS FIVE OR SIX DOLLARS A NIGHT - TEN CENTS A HEAD, CHILDREN AND NIGGERS FREE - BUSINESS A-GROWIN' ALL THE TIME -

I WAS THE PET OF THE WOMEN FOLKS, BIG AND LITTLE, FOR I WAS MAKIN' IT MIGHTY WARM FOR THE RUMMIES, I *TELL* YOU.

WHEN SOMEHOW OR ANOTHER A LITTLE REPORT GOT AROUND LAST NIGHT THAT I HAD A WAY OF PUTTIN' IN MY TIME WITH A PRIVATE JUG ON THE SLY.

A NIGGER ROUSTED ME OUT THIS MORNIN', AND TOLD ME THE PEOPLE WAS GETHERIN' ON THE QUIET WITH THEIR DOGS AND HORSES. I DIDN'T WAIT FOR NO BREAKFAST!

WHAT'S YOUR LINE - MAINLY?

I AIN'T UNDISPOSED.

OLD MAN, I RECKON WE MIGHT DOUBLE-TEAM IT TOGETHER; WHAT DO YOU THINK?

74

TAKE A TURN TO MESMERISM AND PHRENOLOGY WHEN THERE'S A CHANCE; TEACH SINGING-GEOGRAPHY SCHOOL FOR A CHANGE; SLING A LECTURE SOMETIMES –

JOUR PRINTER BY TRADE; DO A LITTLE IN PATENT MEDICINES; THEATER-ACTOR – TRAGEDY, YOU KNOW;

I DO LOTS OF THINGS – MOST ANYTHING THAT COMES HANDY, SO IT AIN'T WORK. WHAT'S YOUR LAY?

I'VE DONE CONSIDERBLE IN THE DOCTORING WAY IN MY TIME, AND I K'N TELL A FORTUNE PRETTY GOOD WHEN I'VE GOT SOMEBODY ALONG TO FIND OUT THE FACTS FOR ME.

PREACHIN'S MY LINE, TOO, AND WORKIN' CAMP-MEETIN'S AND MISSIONARYIN' AROUND.

THESE TWO ARE RIGHT HUMBUGS...

ALAS!

TO THINK I SHOULD HAVE LIVED TO BE LEADING SUCH A LIFE, AND BE DEGRADED DOWN INTO SUCH COMPANY.

SmmmGH

DERN YOUR SKIN, AIN'T THE COMPANY GOOD ENOUGH FOR YOU?

YES, IT IS GOOD ENOUGH FOR ME.

BROUGHT YOU DOWN FROM WHAR? WHAR WAS YOU BROUGHT DOWN FROM?

IT'S AS GOOD AS I DESERVE!

FOR WHO FETCHED ME SO LOW WHEN I WAS SO HIGH? I DID MYSELF. I BROUGHT MYSELF DOWN.

GENTLEMEN, I WILL REVEAL IT TO YOU, FOR I FEEL I MAY HAVE CONFIDENCE IN YOU.

HERE AM I, FORLORN, TORN FROM MY HIGH ESTATE, HUNTED OF MEN, DESPISED BY THE COLD WORLD, RAGGED, WORN, HEART-BROKEN, AND DEGRADED TO THE COMPANIONSHIP OF FELONS ON A RAFT!

WHAT?

BUT BY RIGHTS I AM A DUKE!

NO! YOU CAN'T MEAN IT?

YES. MY GREAT-GRANDFATHER, ELDEST SON OF THE DUKE OF BRIDGEWATER, FLED TO THIS COUNTRY ABOUT THE END OF THE LAST CENTURY, TO BREATHE THE PURE AIR OF FREEDOM; MARRIED HERE, AND DIED, LEAVING A SON.

THE SECOND SON, HIS BROTHER, SEIZED THE TITLES AND ESTATES - THE INFANT REAL DUKE WAS IGNORED.

I AM THE LINEAL DESCENDANT OF THAT INFANT - I AM THE RIGHTFUL DUKE OF BRIDGEWATER!

WE TRIED TO COMFORT HIM, BUT HE SAID IT WARN'T MUCH USE.

SAID IF WE WAS TO ACKNOWLEDGE HIM, THAT WOULD DO HIM MORE GOOD THAN MOST ANYTHING ELSE.

AND SAY "YOUR GRACE" OR "YOUR LORDSHIP". AND ONE OF YOU OUGHT TO WAIT ON ME AT DINNER -

TELL US HOW?

LOOKY HERE!

WELL, YOU OUGHT TO BOW WHEN YOU SPEAK TO ME.

BILGEWATER, I'M NATION SORRY FOR YOU, BUT YOU AIN'T THE ONLY PERSON THAT'S HAD TROUBLES LIKE THAT.

YOU AIN'T THE ONLY PERSON THAT'S HAD A SECRET OF HIS BIRTH!

HOLD! WHAT DO YOU MEAN?

BILGEWATER, KIN I TRUST YOU?

TO THE BITTER DEATH! THAT SECRET OF YOUR BEING: SPEAK!

BILGEWATER, I AM THE LATE DAUPHIN!

YOUR EYES IS LOOKIN' AT THIS VERY MOMENT ON THE PORE DISAPPEARED DAUPHIN, LOOY THE SEVENTEEN, SON OF LOOY THE SIXTEEN AND MARRY ANTONETTE.

SHOCK-

YOU ARE WHAT?

179

TROUBLE HAS DONE IT, BILGEWATER, TROUBLE HAS DONE IT. TROUBLE HAS BRUNG THESE GRAY HAIRS AND THIS PREMATURE BALDITUDE.

YOU! AT YOUR AGE! NO!

YES, GENTLEMEN, YOU SEE BEFORE YOU, IN BLUE JEANS AND MISERY, THE WANDERIN', EXILED, TRAMPLED-ON, AND SUFFERIN' RIGHTFUL KING OF FRANCE.

EVEN I AM DEGRADED TO HAVE THE LAYMAN AS MY COMPANY, BUT THE KING'S BLOOD IS STILL RUNNING INSIDE ME.

IT OFTEN MAKES ME FEEL EASIER AND BETTER FOR A WHILE IF PEOPLE TREAT ME ACCORDING TO MY RIGHTS.

WELL, NOW, WE IS SO SORRY.

HOW?

WELL, YOU GET DOWN ON ONE KNEE TO SPEAK TO ME, AND ALWAYS CALL ME "YOUR MAJESTY"...

AND WAIT ON ME FIRST AT MEALS, AND DON'T SET DOWN IN MY PRESENCE TIL I ASK YOU...

...

BILGEWATER,

LIKE AS NOT WE GOT TO BE TOGETHER A BLAMED LONG TIME ON THIS H-YER RAFT, AND SO WHAT'S THE USE O' YOUR BEIN' SOUR?

COME, GIVE US YOUR HAND, DUKE, AND LE'S ALL BE FRIENDS.

THE DUKE DONE IT, AND JIM AND ME WAS PRETTY GLAD TO SEE IT.

IT TOOK AWAY ALL THE UNCOMFORTABLENESS AND WE FELT MIGHTY GOOD OVER IT, BECAUSE IT WOULD A BEEN A MISERABLE BUSINESS TO HAVE ANY UNFRIENDLINESS ON THE RAFT.

BUT I NEVER SAID NOTHING, NEVER LET ON; KEPT IT TO MYSELF; IT'S THE BEST WAY; THEN YOU DON'T HAVE NO QUARRELS, AND DON'T GET INTO NO TROUBLE.

IT DIDN'T TAKE ME LONG TO MAKE UP MY MIND THAT THESE LIARS WARN'T NO KINGS NOR DUKES AT ALL, BUT JUST LOW-DOWN FRAUDS.

IF I NEVER LEARNT NOTHING ELSE OUT OF PAP,

I LEARNT THAT THE BEST WAY TO GET ALONG WITH HIS KIND OF PEOPLE IS TO LET THEM HAVE THEIR OWN WAY.

CHAPTER XX

SIIIGH

THEY ASKED US CONSIDERABLE MANY QUESTIONS; WANTED TO KNOW WHAT WE COVERED UP THE RAFT THAT WAY FOR, AND LAID BY IN THE DAYTIME INSTEAD OF RUNNING – WAS JIM A RUNAWAY NIGGER?

I HAD TO ACCOUNT FOR THINGS SOME WAY, SO I MADE UP A YARN ON THE SPOT.

I TOLD THEM ABOUT HOW PEOPLE WAS ALWAYS TRYING TO TAKE JIM AWAY FROM ME ON ACCOUNT OF THEY BELIEVED HE WAS A RUNAWAY.

THE DUKE THOUGHT THE THING OVER AND SAID HE CIPHERED OUT A WAY TO RUN IN THE DAYTIME.

WE DON'T RUN DAYTIMES NO MORE NOW; NIGHTS THEY DON'T BOTHER US.

THE KING ALLOWED HE WOULD GO, TOO, AND SEE IF HE COULDN'T STRIKE SOMETHING.

THERE WAS A LITTLE ONE-HORSE TOWN ABOUT THREE MILE DOWN THE BEND, AND THE DUKE ALLOWED HE WOULD GO DOWN TO THE TOWN AND FIX THAT WAY HE'D CIPHERED.

WE WAS OUT OF COFFEE, SO JIM SAID I BETTER GO ALONG WITH THEM IN THE CANOE AND GET SOME.

SHUFF

WHEN WE GOT THERE THERE WARN'T NOBODY STIRRING; STREETS EMPTY, AND PERFECTLY DEAD AND STILL, LIKE SUNDAY.

WE WAS TOLD THAT EVERYBODY THAT WARN'T TOO YOUNG OR TOO SICK OR TOO OLD WAS GONE TO CAMP-MEETING.

THE KING GOT THE DIRECTIONS, AND ALLOWED HE'D GO AND WORK THAT CAMP-MEETING FOR ALL IT WAS WORTH, AND I MIGHT GO, TOO.

HEH

SO WE LIT OUT FOR THE CAMP-MEETING.

THE FIRST I KNOWED THE KING GOT A-GOING, AND HE WENT A-CHARGING UP ON TO THE PLATFORM – HE TOLD THEM HE WAS A PIRATE – BEEN A PIRATE FOR THIRTY YEARS OUT IN THE INDIAN OCEAN –

AND HE WAS A CHANGED MAN NOW, AND HAPPY FOR THE FIRST TIME IN HIS LIFE, AND, POOR AS HE WAS, HE WAS GOING TO START RIGHT OFF AND WORK HIS WAY BACK TO THE INDIAN OCEAN, AND PUT IN THE REST OF HIS LIFE TRYING TO TURN THE PIRATES INTO THE TRUE PATH...

AND THEN HE BUSTED INTO TEARS...

CRY

SOB

SNIVEL

AND SO DID EVERYBODY.

AND THEN SOMEBODY SINGS OUT, "TAKE UP A COLLECTION FOR HIM!"

OHHHH –

HAHAHAHA!

TODAY I'VE COLLECTED EIGHTY-SEVEN DOLLARS AND SEVENTY-FIVE CENTS!

TAKE IT ALL AROUND, IT LAYS OVER ANY DAY I'VE EVER PUT IN IN THE MISSIONARYING LINE!

THEY WAS INVITING HIM TO LIVE IN THEIR HOUSES, AND STAY A WEEK, AND THEY'D THINK IT WAS AN HONOR...

FETCHED AWAY A THREE-GALLON JUG OF WHISKY, TOO, THAT I FOUND UNDER A WAGON WHEN I WAS STARTING HOME...

HA HA HA

HE REALLY WORKED THAT CAMP-MEETING WITH THOSE PIRATES!

186

AHEM!

I THOUGHT I'D DONE PRETTY WELL TILL THE KING COME TO SHOW UP!

LOOK AT THIS LITTLE JOB.

I HAIN'T CHARGED NOTHIN' FOR THIS ONE, BECAUSE IT'S FOR US.

I TOOK IN NINE DOLLARS AND A HALF FROM THE PRINTER'S OFFICE, BUT AFTER THAT I DON'T THINK SO MUCH OF IT.

FLAP

$200 REWARD

WHENEVER WE SEE ANYBODY COMING WE CAN TIE JIM HAND AND FOOT WITH A ROPE, AND LAY HIM IN THE WIGWAM AND SHOW THIS HANDBILL AND SAY WE CAPTURED HIM UP THE RIVER.

A PICTURE OF A RUNAWAY NIGGER? WAIT. THIS IS TALKING ABOUT JIM!

"$200 REWARD"?

WE CAN SAY WE GOT THIS LITTLE RAFT ON CREDIT FROM OUR FRIENDS AND ARE GOING DOWNSTREAM TO GET THE REWARD!

GOOD JOB, BILGEWATER!

HUCK, DOES YOU RECK'N WE GWYNE TO RUN ACROST ANY MO' KINGS ON DIS TRIP?

NO, I RECKON NOT.

WELL, DAT'S ALL RIGHT, DEN. I DOAN' MINE ONE ER TWO KINGS, BUT DAT'S ENOUGH.

HA HA HA HA

HAHA...

$200 REWARD

$200 RE

WELL, YOU DONE IT PRETTY WELL.

ONLY YOU MUSTN'T BELLOW OUT *ROMEO!* THAT WAY, LIKE A BULL.

CHAPTER XXI

YOU MUST SAY IT SOFT AND SICK AND LANGUISHY - JULIET'S A DEAR SWEET MERE CHILD OF A GIRL, YOU KNOW, AND SHE DOESN'T BRAY LIKE A JACKASS.

R-R-R-O.. ME..O...

SO - R-O-O-MEO!

WELL, CAPET, WE'LL WANT A LITTLE SOMETHING TO ANSWER ENCORES WITH.

THE DUKE HAD TO LEARN THE KING OVER AND OVER AGAIN HOW TO SAY EVERY SPEECH.

LET ME SEE - OH, I'VE GOT IT - YOU CAN DO HAMLET'S SOLILOQUY.

I RECKON I CAN PIECE THAT OUT FROM MEMORY.

AHEM-HEM!

TO BE, OR NOT TO BE; THAT IS THE BARE BODKIN

THAT MAKES CALAMITY OF SO LONG LIFE;

HE JUST KNOCKED THE SPOTS OUT OF ANY ACTING EVER I SEE BEFORE. IT WAS PERFECTLY LOVELY THE WAY HE WOULD RIP AND TEAR AND RAIR UP BEHIND WHEN HE WAS GETTING IT OFF.

AND MAKES US RATHER SLING THE ARROWS OF OUTRAGEOUS FORTUNE

THAN FLY TO OTHERS THAT WE KNOW NOT OF!

ONE MORNING, WHEN WE WAS PRETTY WELL DOWN THE STATE OF ARKANSAW, WE COME IN SIGHT OF A LITTLE ONE-HORSE TOWN IN A BIG BEND; SO WE TIED UP ABOUT THREE-QUARTERS OF A MILE ABOVE IT.

BRICKSVILLE, ARKANSAS

THE DUKE HE HIRED THE COURT HOUSE, AND WE WENT AROUND AND STUCK UP OUR BILLS.

ALL OF US BUT JIM TOOK THE CANOE AND WENT DOWN THERE.

MNCH MNCH

THEN WE WENT LOAFING AROUND THE TOWN.

ALL THE STORES WAS ALONG ONE STREET. THERE WAS LOAFERS ROOSTING IN FRONT OF THEM ALL DAY LONG – A MIGHTY ORNERY LOT.

RABBLE

WAAAAW

RABBLE

LONG ABOUT NOON THIS FELLOW NAMED BOGGS COMES A-TEARING ALONG ON HIS HORSE, DRUNK, AND WEAVING ABOUT IN HIS SADDLE.

EVERYBODY YELLED AT HIM AND LAUGHED AT HIM AND SASSED HIM, AND HE SASSED BACK.

ANYWAY, THEN HE RODE UP BEFORE THE BIGGEST STORE IN TOWN AND STARTS YELLING ABOUT A FELLOW NAME OF COLONEL SHERBURN.

BY AND BY COLONEL SHERBURN STEPS OUT OF THE STORE.

HE SAYS TO BOGGS, MIGHTY CA'M AND SLOW - HE SAYS:

I'M TIRED OF THIS, BUT I'LL ENDURE IT TILL ONE O'CLOCK. TILL ONE O'CLOCK, MIND - NO LONGER.

THE CROWD LOOKED MIGHTY SOBER AT THAT; NOBODY STIRRED, AND THERE WARN'T NO MORE LAUGHING.

SALOON

IN ABOUT FIVE OR TEN MINUTES HERE COMES BOGGS AGAIN, A-REELING ACROSS THE STREET. HE WAS QUIET, BUT THAT DIDN'T MAKE NO DIFFERENCE TO COLONEL SHERBURN.

BANG!

PRETTY SOON THE WHOLE TOWN WAS THERE, SQUIRMING AND SCROUGING AND PUSHING AND SHOVING TO GET AT THE WINDOW AND HAVE A LOOK.

MURMUR

MURMUR

THEY TOOK BOGGS TO A LITTLE DRUG STORE, THE CROWD PRESSING AROUND JUST THE SAME, AND THE WHOLE TOWN FOLLOWING.

WELL, BY AND BY SOMEBODY SAID SHERBURN OUGHT TO BE LYNCHED. IN ABOUT A MINUTE EVERYBODY WAS SAYING IT.

CHAPTER XXII

THEY SWARMED UP TOWARDS SHERBURN'S HOUSE, A-WHOOPING AND RAGING, AND EVERYTHING HAD TO CLEAR THE WAY OR GET RUN OVER AND TROMPED TO MUSH.

IT WAS AWFUL TO SEE. LOTS OF THE WOMEN AND GIRLS WAS CRYING AND TAKING ON, SCARED MOST TO DEATH.

BOOOO

RAAAAR

SHERBURN

BOO

SHERBURN STEPS OUT ON TO THE ROOF OF HIS LITTLE FRONT PORCH – JUST STOOD THERE, LOOKING DOWN.

SHERBURN RUN HIS EYE SLOW ALONG THE CROWD.

194

COWARDS. IT'S AMUSING. THE IDEA OF YOU THINKING YOU HAD PLUCK ENOUGH TO LYNCH A *MAN.*

I COULD A STAYED IF I WANTED TO, BUT I DIDN'T WANT TO.

NOW *LEAVE.*

THE PEOPLE TRIED A LITTLE TO OUT-GAZE HIM, BUT THEY COULDN'T THEY DROPPED THEIR EYES AND LOOKED SNEAKY.

THE CROWD WASHED BACK SUDDEN, AND THEN BROKE ALL APART, AND WENT TEARING OFF EVERY WHICH WAY.

WELL, THAT NIGHT WE HAD OUR SHOW; BUT THERE WARN'T ONLY ABOUT TWELVE PEOPLE THERE - JUST ENOUGH TO PAY EXPENSES.

AND MAYBE SOMETHING RUTHER WORSE THAN LOW COMEDY, HE RECKONED.

HE SAID HE COULD SIZE THEIR STYLE.

THE DUKE SAID THESE ARKANSAW LUNKHEADS COULDN'T COME UP TO SHAKESPEARE; WHAT THEY WANTED WAS LOW COMEDY.

HMPH!

AT THE COURT HOUSE!
FOR 3 NIGHTS ONLY

THE WORLD-RENOWNED TRAGEDIANS

DAVID GARRICK THE YOUNGER!
AND
EDMUND KEAN THE ELDER!

*OF THE LONDON AND CONTINENTAL
THEATRES,*
IN THEIR THRILLING TRAGEDY OF

THE KING'S CAMELOPARD
OR
THE ROYAL NONESUCH!!!

ADMISSION 50 CENTS.

AT THE BOTTOM WAS THE BIGGEST LINE OF ALL:

*LADIES AND CHILDREN
NOT ADMITTED.*

THE DUKE SAID THAT IF THAT LINE DON'T FETCH 'EM, HE DON'T KNOW ARKANSAW.

ALL DAY THE DUKE AND THE KING WAS HARD AT IT, RIGGING UP A STAGE AND A CURTAIN AND A ROW OF CANDLES FOR FOOTLIGHTS.

THE HOUSE GOT JAM FULL OF MEN IN NO TIME.

CHAPTER XXII

THE NEXT NIGHT

MURMUR

MURMUR

TONIGHT I COME TO YOU TO PRAISE UP THIS TRAGEDY WHAT YOU ARE ABOUT TO SEE. IT IS THE MOST THRILLINGEST TRAGEDY WHAT EVER WAS, WITH THE MAIN PRINCIPAL PART PLAYED BY EDMUND KEAN THE ELDER HIS OWN SELF!

GOOD EVENING, GENTLEMEN.

THAT DUKE SURE CAN GO ON A-BRAGGING...

ROLL UP THE CURTAIN!

SWSH

MWAH-!

SPPF!

HA HA HA

MWAH MWAH MWAH

WIGGLE

THANK YOU, THANK YOU!

SWSH

THIS GREAT TRAGEDY WILL BE PERFORMED ONLY TWO NIGHTS MORE, ON ACCOUNTS OF PRESSING LONDON ENGAGEMENTS, WHERE THE SEATS IS ALL SOLD ALREADY FOR IT IN DRURY LANE!

I HOPE WE HAVE SUCCEEDED IN PLEASING YOU AND INSTRUCTING YOU!

I WOULD BE DEEPLY OBLEEGED IF YOU WILL MENTION IT TO YOUR FRIENDS AND GET THEM TO COME AND SEE THE TRAGEDY!

TAK TAK TAK TAK

GET 'EM!

I'M A-GOING FOR THEM TRAGEDIANS!

WE WAS SOLD! THIS IS A FIDDLE!

WHAT, IS IT OVER?

IS THAT ALL?

SOLD!

HOLD ON! JUST A WORD, GENTLEMEN.

WE ARE SOLD – MIGHTY BADLY SOLD. BUT WE DON'T WANT TO BE THE LAUGHING STOCK OF THIS WHOLE TOWN, I RECKON.

NO. WHAT WE WANT IS TO GO OUT OF HERE QUIET, AND TALK THIS SHOW UP, AND SELL THE REST OF THE TOWN!

EH? TH' JEDGE...

THEN WE'LL ALL BE IN THE SAME BOAT. AIN'T THAT SENSIBLE?

THE JEDGE IS RIGHT!

YOU BET IT IS!

GO ALONG HOME, AND ADVISE EVERYBODY TO COME AND SEE THE TRAGEDY.

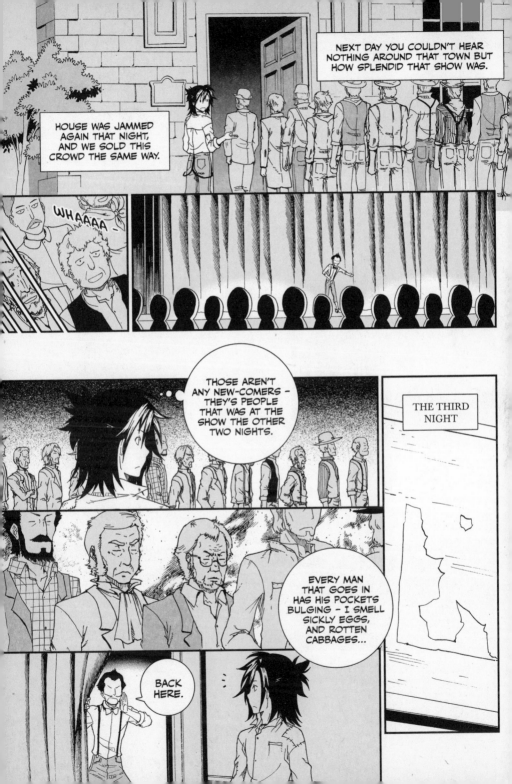

NEXT DAY YOU COULDN'T HEAR NOTHING AROUND THAT TOWN BUT HOW SPLENDID THAT SHOW WAS.

HOUSE WAS JAMMED AGAIN THAT NIGHT, AND WE SOLD THIS CROWD THE SAME WAY.

WHAAAAA-

THOSE AREN'T ANY NEW-COMERS - THEY'S PEOPLE THAT WAS AT THE SHOW THE OTHER TWO NIGHTS.

THE THIRD NIGHT

EVERY MAN THAT GOES IN HAS HIS POCKETS BULGING - I SMELL SICKLY EGGS, AND ROTTEN CABBAGES...

BACK HERE.

TOO VARIOUS FOR ME OUT THERE.

?...!

GO!

I GOT A MAN TO TEND THE DOOR FOR ME FOR A MINUTE, BUT WE AIN'T GOT LONG.

OUT THE BACK, QUICK. WALK FAST TILL YOU GET AWAY FROM THE HOUSES, AND THEN SHIN FOR THE RAFT LIKE THE DICKENS WAS AFTER YOU!

WE STRUCK THE RAFT AT THE SAME TIME, AND IN LESS THAN TWO SECONDS WE WAS GLIDING DOWN STREAM, ALL DARK AND STILL, AND EDGING TOWARDS THE MIDDLE OF THE RIVER, NOBODY SAYING A WORD.

I DONE IT, AND HE DONE THE SAME.

WHOOSH!

NO!

FO' HUND'D EN SIXTY-FIVE DOLLARS!?

HUSH! LET'S DON'T WAKE THEM.

THEY'D FAIRLY LAUGHED THEIR BONES LOOSE OVER THE WAY THEY'D SERVED THEM PEOPLE.

NO...

THEY KNEW THE FIRST HOUSE WOULD KEEP MUM AND LET THE REST OF THE TOWN GET ROPED IN; AND THEY KNEW THE TOWN'D LAY FOR THEM THE THIRD NIGHT, AND CONSIDER IT WAS *THEIR* TURN NOW.

WELL, IT *WAS* THE TOWN'S TURN, ONLY WE DIDN'T STAY FOR IT. MAYBE THEY COULD TURN IT INTO A PICNIC – THEY BROUGHT PLENTY PROVISIONS.

DON'T IT S'PRISE YOU DE WAY DEM KINGS CARRIES ON, HUCK?

NO, IT DON'T.

BUT, HUCK, DESE KINGS O' OURN IS REGLAR RAPSCALLIONS.

WELL, THAT'S WHAT I'M A-SAYING; ALL KINGS IS MOSTLY RAPSCALLIONS, AS FUR AS I CAN MAKE OUT.

YOU READ ABOUT THEM ONCE – YOU'LL SEE.

LOOK AT HENRY THE EIGHT; THIS 'N 'S A SUNDAY-SCHOOL SUPERINTENDENT TO *HIM.*

HE USED TO MARRY A NEW WIFE EVERY DAY, AND CHOP OFF HER HEAD NEXT MORNING.

WELL, HENRY HE TAKES A NOTION HE WANTS TO GET UP SOME TROUBLE WITH THIS COUNTRY.. HOW DOES HE GO AT IT?

ALL OF A SUDDEN HE HEAVES ALL THE TEA IN BOSTON HARBOR OVERBOARD!

AND WHACKS OUT A DECLARATION OF INDEPENDENCE, AND DARES THEM TO COME ON.

THAT'S THE KIND OF A BUG HENRY WAS; AND IF WE'D A HAD HIM ALONG 'STEAD OF OUR KINGS HE'D A FOOLED THAT TOWN A HEAP WORSE THAN OURN DONE.

I DON'T SAY THAT OURN IS LAMBS, BECAUSE THEY AIN'T, WHEN YOU COME RIGHT DOWN TO THE COLD FACTS; BUT THEY AIN'T NOTHING TO THAT OLD RAM, ANYWAY.

ALL I SAY IS, KINGS IS KINGS, AND YOU GOT TO MAKE ALLOWANCES. TAKE THEM ALL AROUND, THEY'RE A MIGHTY ORNERY LOT. IT'S THE WAY THEY'RE RAISED.

OH.

YES, A DUKE'S DIFFERENT. BUT NOT VERY DIFFERENT.

NOW DE DUKE, HE'S A TOLERBLE LIKELY MAN IN SOME WAYS.

WELL, ANYWAYS, I DOAN' HANKER FOR NO MO' UN UM, HUCK. DESE IS ALL I KIN STAN'.

IT'S THE WAY I FEEL, TOO, JIM.

BUT WE'VE GOT THEM ON OUR HANDS, AND WE GOT TO REMEMBER WHAT THEY ARE, AND MAKE ALLOWANCES.

SOMETIMES I WISH WE COULD HEAR OF A COUNTRY THAT'S OUT OF KINGS.

I WENT TO SLEEP AFTER THAT.

JIM DIDN'T CALL ME WHEN IT WAS MY TURN.

FLAP

HE OFTEN DONE THAT.

PO' LITTLE 'LIZABETH! PO' LITTLE JOHNNY!

CRCKL

HE WAS THINKING ABOUT HIS WIFE AND HIS CHILDREN, AWAY UP YONDER, AND HE WAS LOW AND HOMESICK.

I DO BELIEVE HE CARED JUST AS MUCH FOR HIS PEOPLE AS WHITE FOLKS DOES FOR THEIR'N.

WHAT MAKES ME FEEL SO BAD DIS TIME 'UZ BEKASE I HEAR SUMPN OVER YONDER ON DE BANK LIKE A WHACK, WHILE AGO, EN IT MINE ME ER DE TIME I TREAT MY LITTLE 'LIZABETH SO ORNERY.

IT'S MIGHTY HARD; I SPEC' I AIN'T EVER GWYNE TO SEE THEM NO MO', NO MO'!

SHE WARN'T ON'Y 'BOUT FO' YEAR OLE, EN SHE TUCK DE SK'YARLET FEVER,

EN HAD A POWFUL ROUGH SPELL; BUT SHE GOT WELL,

EN ONE DAY SHE WAS A-STANNIN' AROUN', EN I SAYS TO HER, I SAYS: "SHET DE DO'."

IT MAKE ME MAD; EN I SAYS AGIN, MIGHTY LOUD, I SAYS: "DOAN' YOU HEAR ME? SHET DE DO'!" EN WID DAT I FETCH' HER A SLAP SIDE DE HEAD DAT SONT HER A-SPRAWLIN'.

SHE NEVER DONE IT; JIS' STOOD DAH, KINER SMILIN' UP AT ME.

DEN I WENT INTO DE YUTHER ROOM, EN 'UZ GONE 'BOUT TEN MINUTES; EN WHEN I COME BACK DAH WAS DAT DO' A-STANNIN' OPEN YIT, EN DAT CHILE STANNIN' MOS' RIGHT IN IT, A-LOOKIN' DOWN AND MOURNIN'.

WAA

WAA

JIS' DEN, 'LONG COME DE WIND EN SLAM DE DO', BEHINE DE CHILE, KER-BLAM! - EN MY LAN', DE CHILE NEVER MOVE'!

MY BREFF MOS' HOP OUTER ME.

210

I CROPE OUT, ALL A-TREMBLIN', EN CROPE AROUN' EN OPEN DE DO' EASY EN SLOW...

EN POKE MY HEAD IN BEHINE DE CHILE, SOF' EN STILL, EN ALL UV A SUDDEN I SAYS POW! JIS' AS LOUD AS I COULD YELL.

SHE NEVER BUDGE!

EN SAY, "OH, DE PO' LITTLE THING! DE LORD GOD AMIGHTY FOGIVE PO' OLE JIM!"

"KAZE HE NEVER GWYNE TO FOGIVE HISSELF AS LONG'S HE LIVE!"

I BUST OUT A-CRYIN' EN GRAB HER UP IN MY ARMS.

OH, SHE WAS PLUMB DEEF EN DUMB, HUCK, PLUMB DEEF EN DUMB –

EN I'D BEN A-TREAT'N HER SO!

DE PO' CHILE...

PO' CHILE...

AROO!

AROOO!

AROOOOOO!

AROOOOOO!

THE NEXT DAY

CHAPTER XXIV

WELL DONE, 'SICK ARAB'! NOW MAKE YOURSELF FREE AND EASY IN THAT GOWN AND BLUE PAINT.

DAT'S A SIGHT BETTER DEN BEFO'.

WISH WE COULD TRY THE NONESUCH AGAIN. THERE'S SO MUCH MONEY IN IT.

IF ANYBODY EVER COME MEDDLING AROUND, HOP OUT OF THE WIGWAM, AND CARRY ON A LITTLE, AND FETCH A HOWL OR TWO LIKE A WILD BEAST. LIKE AS NOT THEY'LL LIGHT OUT AND LEAVE YOU ALONE.

213

RECKON I'LL DROP OVER TO T'OTHER VILLAGE WITHOUT A PLAN, AND JUST TRUST IN PROVIDENCE TO LEAD ME THE PROFITABLE WAY.

PUT ON YOUR STORE CLOTHES, HUCKLEBERRY, AND MAKE LIKE YOU'RE MY SERVANT.

ALL RIGHT.

MEANING THE DEVIL, I'D RECKON.

PRETTY SOON WE COME TO A NICE INNOCENT-LOOKING YOUNG COUNTRY JAKE; HE HAD A COUPLE OF BIG CARPET-BAGS BY HIM.

I FETCHED THE SHORE A HALF A MILE ABOVE THE VILLAGE, AND THEN WENT SCOOTING ALONG THE BLUFF BANK IN THE EASY WATER.

YES, IT'S POWERFUL WARM TODAY.

MUST BE TOUGH WORK TOTING YOUR BAGGAGE IN SUCH WEATHER.

WHAT ARE YOU THANKING HIM FOR? I'M THE ONE TOTED YOUR BAGS!

I'M MIGHTY THANKFUL FOR YOUR HELP.

BUT I NEVER KNOWED HOW CLOTHES COULD CHANGE A BODY BEFORE.

HEH

HEH HEH

BEFORE THE KING LOOKED LIKE THE ORNERIEST OLD RIP THAT EVER WAS; BUT NOW HE LOOKS THAT GRAND AND GOOD AND PIOUS THAT YOU'D SAY HE HAD WALKED RIGHT OUT OF THE ARK!

WE'RE GOING UP A FEW MILE TO SEE AN OLD FRIEND.

215

WHEN I FIRST SEE YOU I SAYS TO MYSELF, "IT'S MR. WILKS, SURE, AND HE COME MIGHTY NEAR GETTING HERE IN TIME." BUT THEN I SAYS AGAIN, "NO, I RECKON IT AIN'T HIM."

YOU AIN'T HIM, ARE YOU?

NO, MY NAME'S BLODGETT - ELEXANDER BLODGETT - REVEREND ELEXANDER BLODGETT. HOW'D YOU FIGURE?

MR. WILKS WOULDN'T BE PADDLING UP THE RIVER.

WELL, I'M SORRY FOR MR. WILKS FOR NOT ARRIVING IN TIME, ALL THE SAME, IF HE'S MISSED ANYTHING BY IT - WHICH I HOPE HE HASN'T.

TOO BAD, TOO BAD.

WELL, HE DON'T MISS ANY PROPERTY BY IT, BECAUSE HE'LL GET THAT ALL RIGHT; BUT HE'S MISSED SEEING HIS BROTHER PETER DIE.

OH, YES; A MONTH OR TWO AGO, WHEN PETER WAS FIRST TOOK. HE MOST DESPERATELY WANTED TO SEE HARVEY - AND WILLIAM, TOO, FOR THAT MATTER.

DID ANYBODY SEND HIM WORD?

WILLIAM'S THE YOUNGEST BROTHER - HE'S THE DEEF AND DUMB ONE - WILLIAM AIN'T MORE THAN THIRTY OR THIRTY-FIVE.

WILLIAM?

PETER AND GEORGE WERE THE ONLY ONES THAT COME OUT HERE.

PETER HADN'T SEEN HARVEY SINCE THEY WAS BOYS TOGETHER, AND HADN'T EVER SEEN HIS BROTHER WILLIAM AT ALL!

HARVEY AND WILLIAM STILL LIVE IN ENGLAND - SHEFFIELD - HARVEY PREACHES THERE - HASN'T EVER BEEN IN THIS COUNTRY.

GEORGE WAS THE MARRIED BROTHER; HIM AND HIS WIFE HAD THREE G'YIRLS. HIM AND HIS WIFE BOTH DIED LAST YEAR.

PETER LEFT A LETTER BEHIND FOR HARVEY, AND SAID HE'D TOLD IN IT WHERE HIS MONEY WAS HID, AND HOW HE WANTED THE REST OF THE PROPERTY DIVIDED UP SO GEORGE'S G'YIRLS WOULD BE ALL RIGHT - FOR GEORGE DIDN'T LEAVE NOTHING.

WAS PETER WILKS WELL OFF?

OH, YES, PRETTY WELL OFF. HE HAD HOUSES AND LAND, AND IT'S RECKONED HE LEFT THREE OR FOUR THOUSAND IN CASH HID UP SOM'ERS.

WELL, THE OLD MAN WENT ON ASKING QUESTIONS TILL HE JUST FAIRLY EMPTIED THAT YOUNG FELLOW.

BLAMED IF HE DIDN'T INQUIRE ABOUT EVERYBODY AND EVERYTHING IN THAT BLESSED TOWN, AND ALL ABOUT THE WILKSES, AND SO ON, AND SO ON.

I SEE WHAT *HE* WAS UP TO;

BUT I NEVER SAID NOTHING, OF COURSE.

SPLASH SPLASH

WHEN WE STRUCK THE BOAT SHE WAS ABOUT DONE LOADING, AND PRETTY SOON SHE GOT OFF. THE KING TOLD ME TO HUSTLE BACK AND FETCH THE DUKE UP THERE.

WHEN I GOT BACK WITH THE DUKE WE SET DOWN AND THE KING TOLD HIM EVERYTHING, JUST LIKE THE YOUNG FELLOW HAD SAID IT - EVERY LAST WORD OF IT.

THE KING HE WAS ALREADY TRYING TO TALK LIKE AN ENGLISHMAN; AND HE DONE IT PRETTY WELL, TOO, FOR A SLOUCH. THE DUKE SAID HE HAD PLAYED A DEEF AND DUMB PERSON ON THE HISTRONIC BOARDS, SO THEY WAS SET.

SO THEN THEY WAITED FOR A STEAMBOAT.

WHEN WE GOT TO THE VILLAGE THE STEAMBOAT YAWLED US ASHORE.

SOME MEN FLOCKED DOWN WHEN THEY SEE THE YAWL A-COMING, AND SUDDEN AS WINKING THE ORNERY OLD CRETUR WENT AN TO SMASH.

CHAPTER XXV

STEP

SOB

ALAS, ALAS, OUR POOR BROTHER - GONE, AND WE NEVER GOT TO SEE HIM; OH, IT'S TOO, TOO HARD!

SHIVER

SHIVER

WELL, THE MEN GATHERED AROUND AND SYMPATHIZED WITH THEM, AND SAID ALL SORTS OF KIND THINGS TO THEM, AND TOLD THE KING ALL ABOUT HIS BROTHER'S LAST MOMENTS.

IT WAS ENOUGH TO MAKE A BODY ASHAMED OF THE HUMAN RACE.

IF EVER I STRUCK ANYTHING LIKE IT, I'M A NIGGER.

WILKS' HOUSE

THE NEWS WAS ALL OVER TOWN IN TWO MINUTES.

CLING—

THE KING HE SPREAD HIS ARMS, AND TWO OF THE GIRLS THEY JUMPED FOR THEM.

WHEN WE GOT TO THE HOUSE THE THREE GIRLS WAS STANDING IN THE DOOR.

EVERYBODY MOST, LEASTWAYS WOMEN, CRIED FOR JOY TO SEE THEM MEET AGAIN AT LAST AND HAVE SUCH GOOD TIMES.

222

MARY JANE WILKS

SUSAN WILKS

JOANNA WILKS

THE KING AND THE DUKE THEY BENT OVER AND LOOKED IN THE COFFIN, AND TOOK ONE SIGHT

I NEVER SEE TWO MEN LEAK THE WAY THEY DONE.

SNUF

SOB

SOB

SHU...

AND THEN THEY BUST OUT A-CRYING SO YOU COULD A HEARD THEM TO ORLEANS, MOST.

SOB

SOB AHUH

SOB

SNUFFLE

AND, MIND YOU, EVERYBODY WAS DOING THE SAME; AND THE PLACE WAS THAT DAMP I NEVER SEE ANYTHING LIKE IT.

EVERYBODY BROKE DOWN AND WENT TO SOBBING RIGHT OUT LOUD - THE POOR GIRLS, TOO; AND EVERY WOMAN, NEARLY, WENT UP TO THE GIRLS, WITHOUT SAYING A WORD, AND KISSED THEM, SOLEMN, ON THE FOREHEAD

AND THEN LOOKED UP TOWARDS THE SKY, WITH THE TEARS RUNNING DOWN, AND THEN BUSTED OUT AND WENT OFF SOBBING AND SWABBING, AND GIVE THE NEXT WOMAN A SHOW.

WAIL

SOB

SOB

SNUFFLE

I NEVER SEE ANYTHING SO DISGUSTING.

THE KING SAYS HOW HIM AND HIS NIECES WOULD BE GLAD IF A FEW OF THE MAIN PRINCIPAL FRIENDS OF THE FAMILY WOULD TAKE SUPPER HERE WITH THEM THAT EVENING, AND MANAGED TO INQUIRE ABOUT PRETTY MUCH EVERYBODY AND DOG IN TOWN, BY HIS NAME.

WILKS HOUSE

AFTER DINNER, MARY JANE SHE FETCHED THE LETTER HER FATHER LEFT BEHIND, AND THE KING HE READ IT OUT LOUD AND CRIED OVER IT.

FRIENDS ALL...

IT GIVE THE DWELLING-HOUSE AND THREE THOUSAND DOLLARS, GOLD, TO THE GIRLS; AND IT GIVE THE TANYARD ALONG WITH SOME OTHER HOUSES AND LAND AND THREE THOUSAND DOLLARS IN GOLD TO HARVEY AND WILLIAM.

MY POOR BROTHER THAT LAYS YONDER HAS DONE GENEROUS BY THEM THAT'S LEFT BEHIND IN THE VALE OF SORRERS.

AHEM!

HE HAS DONE GENEROUS BY THESE YER POOR LITTLE LAMBS THAT HE LOVED AND SHELTERED, AND THAT'S LEFT FATHERLESS AND MOTHERLESS.

NOW, WOULDN'T HE?

YES, AND WE THAT KNOWED HIM KNOWS THAT HE WOULD A DONE MORE GENEROUS BY 'EM IF HE HADN'T BEN AFEARD O' WOUNDIN' HIS DEAR WILLIAM AND ME.

THER' AIN'T NO QUESTION 'BOUT IT IN MY MIND.

WELL, THEN, WHAT KIND O' BROTHERS WOULD IT BE THAT'D STAND IN HIS WAY AT SECH A TIME?

SIGH.

226

AND WHAT KIND O' UNCLES WOULD IT BE THAT'D ROB - YES, ROB - SECH POOR SWEET LAMBS AS THESE 'AT HE LOVED SO AT SECH A TIME?

IT'S THE GIFT OF HIM THAT LAYS YONDER, COLD BUT JOYFUL.

TAKE THE MONEY - TAKE IT ALL.

IF I KNOW WILLIAM - AND I THINK I DO - HE - WELL, HE'D AGREE.

HERE, MARY JANE, SUSAN, JOANNER.

HOW LOVELY!

OHHH -

YOU DEAR GOOD SOULS!

HOW COULD YOU!

TOMORROW WE WANT ALL TO COME - EVERYBODY; FOR HE RESPECTED EVERYBODY, HE LIKED EVERYBODY, AND SO IT'S FITTEN THAT HIS FUNERAL ORGIES SH'D BE PUBLIC.

WH-

WE WANT TO THANK YOU FOR COMIN' TO DINNER, YOU BEIN' PARTICKLER FRIENDS O' THE DISEASED.

OBSEQUIES, YOU OLD FOOL.

EH?

TAP TAP

POOR WILLIAM, AFFLICTED AS HE IS, HIS HEART'S ALUZ RIGHT.

ASKS ME TO INVITE EVERYBODY TO COME TO THE FUNERAL - IT WAS JEST WHAT I WAS AT.

SHUF

OBSEQUIES AIN'T USED IN ENGLAND NO MORE NOW – IT'S GONE OUT. WE SAY ORGIES NOW IN ENGLAND. ORGIES IS BETTER, BECAUSE IT MEANS THE THING YOU'RE AFTER MORE EXACT.

NOW, I SAY ORGIES, NOT BECAUSE IT'S THE COMMON TERM, BUT BECAUSE ORGIES IS THE RIGHT TERM.

IT'S A WORD THAT'S MADE UP OUT'N THE GREEK ORGO, OUTSIDE, OPEN, ABROAD; AND THE HEBREW JEESUM, TO PLANT, COVER UP; HENCE INTER. SO, YOU SEE, FUNERAL ORGIES IS AN OPEN ER PUBLIC FUNERAL.

HE'S THE WORST I EVER STRUCK!

IS IT MY POOR BROTHER'S DEAR GOOD FRIEND AND PHYSICIAN? I –

WHY, DOCTOR!

HAHAHA!

HA!

KEEP YOUR HANDS OFF OF ME!

DR. ROBINSON

THE DOCTOR UP AND TURNED ON THE GIRLS.

YOU TALK LIKE AN ENGLISHMAN, DON'T YOU?

IT'S THE WORST IMITATION I EVER HEARD. YOU PETER WILKS'S BROTHER!

YOU'RE A FRAUD, THAT'S WHAT YOU ARE!

I WAS YOUR FATHER'S FRIEND, AND I'M YOUR FRIEND; AND I WARN YOU AS A FRIEND.

HE IS THE THINNEST KIND OF AN IMPOSTOR - HAS COME HERE WITH A LOT OF EMPTY NAMES AND FACTS WHICH HE PICKED UP SOMEWHERES, AND YOU TAKES THEM FOR PROOFS.

THIS IGNORANT TRAMP, WITH HIS IDIOTIC GREEK AND HEBREW, AS HE CALLS IT.

HERE IS MY ANSWER.

MARY JANE WILKS, YOU KNOW ME FOR YOUR FRIEND, AND FOR YOUR UNSELFISH FRIEND, TOO.

NOW LISTEN TO ME; TURN THIS PITIFUL RASCAL OUT — I *BEG* YOU TO DO IT. WILL YOU?

WHUMP!

TAKE THIS SIX THOUSAND DOLLARS.

INVEST FOR ME AND MY SISTERS ANY WAY YOU WANT TO, AND DON'T GIVE US NO RECEIPT FOR IT.

ALL RIGHT.

EH EH EH

I WASH MY HANDS OF THE MATTER.

BUT I WARN YOU ALL THAT A TIME'S COMING WHEN YOU'RE GOING TO FEEL SICK WHENEVER YOU THINK OF THIS DAY.

CHAPTER XXVI

CH...

CHEW...

CHEW...

DO YOU GO TO UNCLE HARVEY'S CHURCH, TOO?

WISH SHE WOULDN'T STARE SO...

WHY, IN OUR PEW - YOUR UNCLE HARVEY'S.

WHERE DO YOU SET?

YES - REGULAR.

BLAME IT, DO YOU SUPPOSE THERE AIN'T BUT ONE PREACHER TO A CHURCH?

ROT HIM, I FORGOT HE WAS A PREACHER!

I THOUGHT HE'D BE IN THE PULPIT.

THEY DON'T HAVE NO LESS THAN SEVENTEEN.

Spfft!

WHY, I WOULDN'T SET OUT SUCH A STRING AS THAT, NOT IF I *NEVER* GOT TO GLORY. IT MUST TAKE 'EM A WEEK.

SEVENTEEN! MY LAND!

A SERVANT AIN'T NOBODY THERE. THEY TREAT THEM WORSE THAN DOGS.

THEY NEVER SEE A HOLIDAY FROM YEAR'S END TO YEAR'S END; NEVER GO NOWHERES.

SHUCKS, THEY DON'T ALL OF 'EM PREACH THE SAME DAY - ONLY *ONE* OF 'EM.

NOT EVEN CHURCH?

NOT EVEN CHURCH.

OH. WELL... HOW IS SERVANTS TREATED IN ENGLAND?

HMMM...

I FORGOT I WAS THE OLD MAN'S SERVANT!

BUT *YOU* ALWAYS WENT TO CHURCH.

SPRFFF!

WELL, I'M A VALLEY — IT'S DIFFERENT THAN A COMMON SERVANT. VALLEYS HAS TO GO TO CHURCH WHETHER THEY WANT TO OR NOT —

LAY YOUR HAND ON THIS BOOK AND SAY IT AGAIN!

?

DICTIONARY

DICTIONARY

IF YOU HAIN'T BEEN TELLIN' ME A LOT OF LIES —

DICTIONARY

JOANNA!

IT HAIN'T NOTHING BUT A DICTIONARY...

235

IT AIN'T RIGHT NOR KIND FOR YOU TO TALK SO TO HIM, AND HIM A STRANGER AND SO FAR FROM HIS PEOPLE.

HOW WOULD YOU LIKE TO BE TREATED SO?

THAT'S ALWAYS YOUR WAY, MAIM - ALWAYS SAILING IN TO HELP SOMEBODY BEFORE THEY'RE HURT. I HAIN'T DONE NOTHING TO HIM.

HE'S HERE IN OUR HOUSE AND A STRANGER, AND IT WASN'T GOOD OF YOU TO MAKE HIM FEEL ASHAMED.

WHY, MAIM, HE SAID -

IT DON'T MAKE NO DIFFERENCE WHAT HE *SAID* – THAT AIN'T THE THING.

THE THING IS FOR YOU TO TREAT HIM *KIND*, AND NOT BE SAYING THINGS TO MAKE HIM REMEMBER HE AIN'T IN HIS OWN COUNTRY AND AMONGST HIS OWN FOLKS.

WELL, I HOPE TO GRACIOUS –

ALL RIGHT, THEN.

I SAYS TO MYSELF, *THIS* IS A GIRL THAT I'M LETTING THAT OLD REPTILE ROB HER OF HER MONEY!

PHEW

YOU JUST ASK HIS PARDON.

EH?!

I WISHED I COULD TELL HER A THOUSAND LIES, SO SHE COULD DO IT AGAIN.

SHE DONE IT, TOO; AND SHE DONE IT BEAUTIFUL. SHE DONE IT SO BEAUTIFUL IT WAS GOOD TO HEAR.

THIS IS ANOTHER ONE THAT I'M LETTING HIM ROB HER OF HER MONEY.

I SAYS TO MYSELF,

I'LL HIVE THAT MONEY FOR THEM OR BUST.

I FELT SO ORNERY AND LOW DOWN AND MEAN THAT I SAYS TO MYSELF, MY MIND'S MADE UP.

I SAYS TO MYSELF, SHALL I GO TO THAT DOCTOR, PRIVATE, AND BLOW ON THESE FRAUDS? NO – THAT WON'T DO.

HE MIGHT TELL WHO TOLD HIM; THEN THE KING AND THE DUKE WOULD MAKE IT WARM FOR ME.

THEN I SAYS TO MYSELF, SHALL I GO, PRIVATE, AND TELL MARY JANE? NO – I DASN'T DO IT.

HER FACE WOULD GIVE THEM A HINT, SURE; THEY'VE GOT THE MONEY, AND THEY'D SLIDE RIGHT OUT AND GET AWAY WITH IT.

I'LL STEAL IT AND HIDE IT; AND BY AND BY, WHEN I'M AWAY DOWN THE RIVER, I'LL WRITE A LETTER AND TELL MARY JANE WHERE IT'S HID.

I GOT TO STEAL IT SOME WAY THAT THEY WON'T SUSPICION THAT I DONE IT.

MISS MARY JANE SHE GAVE HER OWN ROOM TO 'UNCLE HARVEY' AND TURNED INTO THE ROOM WITH HER SISTERS.

IT WOULDN'T BE MUCH LIKE THE KING TO LET ANYBODY ELSE TAKE CARE OF THAT MONEY BUT HIS OWN SELF. I'LL PAW AROUND HERE.

SCREE

TAP

TAP
TAP

!

SCREEEE

I HEARS THEIR FOOTSTEPS COMING...

I'LL LAY FOR THEM AND EAVESDROP.

WELL, WHAT IS IT?

AND CUT IT MIDDLIN' SHORT, BECAUSE IT'S BETTER FOR US TO BE DOWN THERE A-WHOOPIN' UP THE MOURNIN' THAN UP HERE GIVIN' 'EM A CHANCE TO TALK US OVER.

WELL, THIS IS IT, CAPET. I AIN'T EASY; I AIN'T COMFORTABLE. I WANTED TO KNOW YOUR PLANS. I'VE GOT A NOTION, AND I THINK IT'S A SOUND ONE.

WHAT IS IT, DUKE?

...

THAT WE BETTER GLIDE OUT OF THIS BEFORE THREE IN THE MORNING, AND CLIP IT DOWN THE RIVER WITH WHAT WE'VE GOT.

SPECIALLY, SEEING WE GOT IT SO EASY - GIVEN BACK TO US, FLUNG AT OUR HEADS, AS YOU MAY SAY, WHEN OF COURSE WE ALLOWED TO HAVE TO STEAL IT BACK.

I'M FOR KNOCKING OFF AND LIGHTING OUT.

!

AND NOT SELL OUT THE REST O' THE PROPERTY?

MARCH OFF LIKE A PASSEL OF FOOLS AND LEAVE EIGHT OR NINE THOUS'N' DOLLARS' WORTH O' PROPERTY LAYIN' AROUND JEST SUFFERIN' TO BE SCOOPED IN?

NO! THAT'D MAKE ME FEEL PRETTY BAD...

WHAT!

THAT BAG OF GOLD IS ENOUGH.

I DON'T WANT TO GO NO DEEPER – DON'T WANT TO ROB A LOT OF ORPHANS OF EVERYTHING THEY HAVE.

WHY, HOW YOU TALK! WE SHA'N'T ROB 'EM OF NOTHING AT ALL BUT JEST THIS MONEY.

THE PEOPLE THAT *BUYS* THE PROPERTY IS THE SUFF'RERS.

AS SOON 'S IT'S FOUND OUT 'AT WE DIDN'T OWN IT – WHICH WON'T BE LONG AFTER WE'VE SLID – THE SALE WON'T BE VALID.

IT'LL ALL GO BACK TO THE ESTATE AND THESE YER ORPHANS 'LL GIT THEIR HOUSE BACK AGIN.

...

ALL RIGHT, I GIVE.

GOOD!

BUT I BELIEVE IT'S BLAMED FOOLISHNESS TO STAY, AND THAT DOCTOR HANGING OVER US.

24

AND AIN'T THAT A BIG ENOUGH MAJORITY IN ANY TOWN?

CUSS THE DOCTOR! WHAT DO WE K'YER FOR HIM?

HAIN'T WE GOT ALL THE FOOLS IN TOWN ON OUR SIDE?

I DON'T THINK WE PUT THAT MONEY IN A GOOD PLACE.

!

WHY?

BECAUSE MARY JANE 'LL BE IN MOURNING FROM THIS OUT; AND FIRST YOU KNOW THE NIGGER THAT DOES UP THE ROOMS WILL GET AN ORDER TO BOX THESE DUDS UP AND PUT 'EM AWAY.

AND DO YOU RECKON A NIGGER CAN RUN ACROSS MONEY AND NOT BORROW SOME OF IT?

YOUR HEAD'S LEVEL AGIN, DUKE.

I'D BEGUN TO THINK I WARN'T GOING TO GET A HINT OF NO KIND!

HE HE HE

SHUFF

THEY'RE SHOVIN' THE BAG THROUGH A RIP IN THE STRAW TICK...

RUSTLE RUSTLE

TIP
TIP
TIP
TIP

I BETTER HIDE IT GOOD, BECAUSE IF THEY MISS IT THEY'LL GIVE THE HOUSE A GOOD RANSACKING.

WHERE CAN I HIDE IT...?

...

CHAPTER XXVII

HEAVY...

FRONT DOOR'S LOCKED...

ONLY PLACE I SEE TO HIDE THE BAG IS THE COFFIN.

SCRAAAAAPE

STEP

STEP

SOMEBODY COMING DOWN THE STAIRS, BACK BEHIND ME!

AAGH, HIS HANDS IS SO COLD!

CLINK

TUCK IT UNDER THE LID, QUICK...

STEP

STEP

STEP

ZIP-

WHO...?

MARY JANE?

TIK

...

SOB... SOB...

HUCK'S ATTIC CUBBY

I SLIPPED UP TO BED, FEELING RUTHER BLUE, ON ACCOUNTS OF THE THING PLAYING OUT THAT WAY AFTER I HAD TOOK SO MUCH TROUBLE AND RUN SO MUCH RESK ABOUT IT.

UGH...

THE THING THAT'S GOING TO HAPPEN IS, THE MONEY 'LL BE FOUND WHEN THEY COME TO SCREW ON THE LID.

THEN THE KING 'LL GET IT AGAIN.

IT'LL BE A LONG DAY BEFORE HE GIVES ANYBODY ANOTHER CHANCE TO SMOUCH IT FROM HIM.

OF COURSE I WANTED TO SLIDE DOWN AND GET IT OUT OF THERE, BUT I DASN'T TRY IT.

THE NEXT AFTERNOON

TOWARDS THE MIDDLE OF THE DAY THE UNDERTAKER COME WITH HIS MAN, AND THEY SET THE COFFIN IN THE MIDDLE OF THE ROOM.

THEN THE PEOPLE BEGUN TO FLOCK IN AND FILE AROUND SLOW, IN SINGLE RANK, AND IT WAS ALL VERY STILL AND SOLEMN.

THEN THE REVEREND HOBSON OPENED UP, SLOW AND SOLEMN.

THE GIRLS AND THE BEATS HELD HANDKERCHIEFS TO THEIR EYES AND KEPT THEIR HEADS BENT, SOBBING A LITTLE.

STRAIGHT OFF THE MOST OUTRAGEOUS ROW BUSTED OUT IN THE CELLAR A BODY EVER HEARD; IT WAS ONLY ONE DOG, BUT HE MADE A MOST POWERFUL RACKET.

WOOF! RUFF!

SNIF

HE DISAPPEARS DOWN CELLAR. THEN IN ABOUT TWO SECONDS THE DOG HE FINISHED UP WITH A MOST AMAZING HOWL OR TWO, AND THEN EVERYTHING WAS DEAD STILL.

PRETTY SOON THAT LONG-LEGGED UNDERTAKER MAKES A SIGN TO THE PREACHER AS MUCH AS TO SAY, "DON'T YOU WORRY - JUST DEPEND ON ME."

THE PARSON HE HAD TO STAND THERE, OVER THE COFFIN, AND WAIT - YOU COULDN'T HEAR YOURSELF THINK.

WOOF! ARF!

OHHH

IN A MINUTE OR TWO HERE COMES THIS UNDERTAKER AGAIN; AND HE SAYS, IN A KIND OF A COARSE WHISPER, "HE HAD A RAT!"

YOU COULD SEE IT WAS A GREAT SATISFACTION TO THE PEOPLE, BECAUSE NATURALLY THEY WANTED TO KNOW.

A LITTLE THING LIKE THAT DON'T COST NOTHING, AND IT'S JUST THE LITTLE THINGS THAT MAKES A MAN TO BE LOOKED UP TO AND LIKED.

THERE WARN'T NO MORE POPULAR MAN IN TOWN THAN WHAT THAT UNDERTAKER WAS.

251

THE KING HE GIVE OUT THE IDEA THAT HIS CONGREGATION OVER IN ENGLAND WOULD BE IN A SWEAT ABOUT HIM, SO HE MUST HURRY AND SETTLE UP THE ESTATE RIGHT AWAY AND LEAVE FOR HOME.

AND HE SAID OF COURSE HIM AND WILLIAM WOULD TAKE THE GIRLS HOME WITH THEM.

THAT PLEASED EVERYBODY IN TOWN, TOO, BECAUSE THEN THE GIRLS WOULD BE WELL FIXED AND AMONGST THEIR OWN RELATIONS.

IT PLEASED THE GIRLS – THEY TOLD HIM TO SELL OUT AS QUICK AS HE WANTED TO, THEY WOULD BE READY.

SO THE NEXT DAY AFTER THE FUNERAL, ALONG ABOUT NOON-TIME, A COUPLE OF NIGGER TRADERS COME ALONG, AND THE KING SOLD THEM THE NIGGERS REASONABLE, THE TWO SONS UP THE RIVER TO MEMPHIS, AND THEIR MOTHER DOWN THE RIVER TO ORLEANS.

WELL, BLAMED IF THE KING DIDN'T BILL THE HOUSE AND THE NIGGERS AND ALL THE PROPERTY FOR AUCTION STRAIGHT OFF.

I THOUGHT THEM POOR GIRLS AND THEM NIGGERS WOULD BREAK THEIR HEARTS FOR GRIEF; THEY CRIED AROUND EACH OTHER, AND TOOK ON SO IT MOST MADE ME DOWN SICK TO SEE IT.

THE THING MADE A BIG STIR IN THE TOWN, TOO, AND A GOOD MANY COME OUT FLATFOOTED AND SAID IT WAS SCANDALOUS TO SEPARATE THE MOTHER AND THE CHILDREN THAT WAY.

IT INJURED THE FRAUDS SOME; BUT THE OLD FOOL HE BULLED RIGHT ALONG, SPITE OF ALL THE DUKE COULD SAY OR DO, AND I TELL YOU THE DUKE WAS POWERFUL UNEASY.

I RECKON I COULDN'T A STOOD IT ALL, BUT WOULD A HAD TO BUST OUT AND TELL ON OUR GANG IF I HADN'T KNOWED THE SALE WARN'T NO ACCOUNT AND THE NIGGERS WOULD BE BACK HOME IN A WEEK OR TWO.

ZZZZ...

?

AUCTION DAY, MORNING

?!

YANK

HONOR BRIGHT, NOW - NO LIES.

WAS YOU IN MY ROOM NIGHT BEFORE LAST?

...?

NO, YOUR MAJESTY.

254

NO, YOUR MAJESTY. HONOR BRIGHT, I'M TELLING YOU THE TRUTH.

WAS YOU IN THERE YISTERDAY ER LAST NIGHT?

THEY'VE FOUND THE BAG GONE, I RECKON.

HAVE YOU SEEN ANYBODY ELSE GO IN THERE?

NO, YOUR GRACE, NOT AS I REMEMBER, I BELIEVE.

STOP AND THINK.

WELL, I SEE THE NIGGERS GO IN THERE SEVERAL TIMES.

WELL, GO ON, GO ON! WHAT DID THEY DO? HOW'D THEY ACT?

THEY DIDN'T DO NOTHING.

HELLO! WHEN WAS THAT?

IT WAS THE DAY WE HAD THE FUNERAL. IN THE MORNING. IT WARN'T EARLY, BECAUSE I OVERSLEPT. I WAS JUST STARTING DOWN THE STAIRS, AND I SEE THEM.

WHUMP

GREAT GUNS, *THIS IS* A GO!

THEY'D SHOVED IN THERE TO DO UP YOUR MAJESTY'S ROOM, OR SOMETHING, S'POSING YOU WAS UP; AND FOUND YOU *WARN'T* UP, SO THEY TIPTOED AWAY.

IT DOES BEAT ALL HOW NEAT THE NIGGERS PLAYED THEIR HAND.

WHUD

THEY LET ON TO BE *SORRY* THEY WAS GOING OUT OF THIS REGION!

AND I BELIEVED THEY *WAS* SORRY, AND SO DID YOU, AND SO DID EVERYBODY.

DON'T EVER TELL *ME* ANY MORE THAT A NIGGER AIN'T GOT ANY HISTRIONIC TALENT.

I WAS TRYING TO DO FOR THE BEST IN SELLIN' 'EM OUT SO QUICK.

THEY'D BE IN THIS HOUSE YET AND WE WOULDN'T IF I COULD A GOT MY ADVICE LISTENED TO.

IS SOMETHING GONE WRONG?

NONE O' YOUR BUSINESS! YOU KEEP YOUR HEAD SHET, AND MIND Y'R OWN AFFAIRS – IF YOU GOT ANY.

AH...

IF THE PROFITS HAS TURNED OUT TO BE NONE, LACKIN' CONSIDABLE, AND NONE TO CARRY, IS IT MY FAULT ANY MORE'N IT'S YOURN?

SO THEY WENT OFF A-JAWING; AND I FELT DREADFUL GLAD I'D WORKED IT ALL OFF ON TO THE NIGGERS, AND YET HADN'T DONE THE NIGGERS NO HARM BY IT.

CHAPTER XXVIII

?

MISS MARY JANE...

CLICK

YOU CAN'T A-BEAR TO SEE PEOPLE IN TROUBLE, AND I CAN'T - MOST ALWAYS.

...

TELL ME ABOUT IT.

I DON'T SEE HOW I CAN BE HAPPY IN ENGLAND.

THIS BEAUTIFUL TRIP IS MOST ABOUT SPOILED FOR ME NOW!

OH, DEAR, DEAR, TO THINK THEY AIN'T EVER GOING TO SEE EACH OTHER ANY MORE!

AND I *KNOW* IT!

BUT THEY *WILL* – AND INSIDE OF TWO WEEKS –

!

GRAB

WHAT?

?

SAY THAT AGAIN!

LAWS, IT WAS OUT BEFORE I COULD THINK!

SAY IT AGAIN, PLEASE, SAY IT *AGAIN*!

SHOCK

WHAT?!

DON'T YOU HOLLER.

THEY'RE FRAUDS?!

IT JOLTED HER UP LIKE EVERYTHING, OF COURSE; BUT I WAS OVER THE SHOAL WATER NOW, SO I WENT RIGHT ALONG.

I TOLD HER EVERY BLAME THING, STARTING FROM WHERE WE FIRST STRUCK THAT YOUNG FOOL GOING UP TO THE STEAMBOAT.

THEN WE WERE OVER THE WORST OF IT AND SHE COULD STAND THE REST MIDDLING EASY.

THE BRUTE!

BUT WHEN I GOT TO THE PART WHERE SHE FLUNG HERSELF ON TO THE KING'S BREAST AT THE FRONT DOOR AND HE KISSED HER SIXTEEN OR SEVENTEEN TIMES...

CLENCH

AND FLUNG IN THE RIVER!

COME, DON'T WASTE A MINUTE - NOT A SECOND -

CERT'NLY.

WE'LL HAVE THEM TARRED AND FEATHERED!

BUT DO YOU MEAN *BEFORE* YOU GO TO MR. LOTHROP'S, OR –

OH, WHAT AM I *THINKING* ABOUT!

I NEVER THOUGHT, I WAS SO STIRRED UP; NOW GO ON, AND I WON'T DO SO ANY MORE.

WELL...

MWAHAHAHA –

I DRUTHER NOT TELL YOU WHY.

IT'S A ROUGH GANG, THEM TWO FRAUDS, AND I'M FIXED SO I GOT TO TRAVEL WITH THEM A WHILE LONGER, WHETHER I WANT TO OR NOT.

I'D BE ALL RIGHT; BUT THERE'D BE ANOTHER PERSON THAT YOU DON'T KNOW ABOUT WHO'D BE IN BIG TROUBLE.

SAYING THEM WORDS PUT A GOOD IDEA IN MY HEAD. I SEE HOW MAYBE I COULD GET ME AND JIM RID OF THE FRAUDS; GET THEM JAILED HERE, AND THEN LEAVE.

I TOLD MISS MARY JANE TO GO ALONG TO MR. LOTHROP'S AND LAY LOW. THERE AIN'T NO BETTER BOOK THAN WHAT HER FACE IS; A BODY COULD SET DOWN AND READ IT OFF LIKE COARSE PRINT.

WELL, WE GOT TO SAVE HIM, HAIN'T WE?

OF COURSE!

IF THE COURT WANTS TO FIND OUT SOMETHING ABOUT THOSE TWO, LET THEM SEND UP TO BRICKSVILLE AND ASK FOR SOME WITNESSES – WHY, THEY'D HAVE THE ENTIRE TOWN DOWN HERE!

I ALSO TOLD HER ABOUT THE ROYAL NONESUCH, AND WROTE THE WORDS DOWN FOR HER TO PUT AWAY.

I TOLD HER TO WAIT TILL ELEVEN, AND IF I DIDN'T TURN UP THEN IT MEANT I WAS GONE, AND OUT OF THE WAY, AND SAFE.

ONCE I WAS GONE SHE SHOULD COME OUT AND SPREAD THE NEWS AROUND, AND GET THESE BEATS JAILED.

SHE LEFT BEFORE BREAKFAST — SHE WAS GLAD TO.

CHIRP CHIRP

I SHA'N'T EVER FORGET YOU AND I'LL THINK OF YOU A MANY AND A MANY A TIME, AND I'LL *PRAY* FOR YOU, TOO!

I DIDN'T WANT TO SET HER THINKING ABOUT HER TROUBLES AGAIN, SO I WROTE WHERE I HID THE BAG OF MONEY ON A PIECE OF PAPER AND TOLD HER SHE COULD READ IT ALONG THE ROAD TO MR. LOTHROP'S.

WHEN IT COMES TO BEAUTY — AND GOODNESS, TOO — SHE LAYS OVER THEM ALL. I HAIN'T EVER SEEN HER SINCE, BUT I RECKON I'VE THOUGHT OF HER A MANY AND A MANY A MILLION TIMES.

CHAPTER XXIX

WELL, THEY HELD THE AUCTION IN THE PUBLIC SQUARE, ALONG TOWARDS THE END OF THE AFTERNOON, AND IT STRUNG ALONG, AND STRUNG ALONG.

THE OLD MAN HE WAS ON HAND AND LOOKING HIS LEVEL PISONEST, UP THERE LONGSIDE OF THE AUCTIONEER.

CHIPPING IN A LITTLE SCRIPTURE NOW AND THEN, OR A LITTLE GOODY-GOODY SAYING OF SOME KIND.

I NEVER SEE SUCH A GIRAFFT AS THE KING WAS FOR WANTING TO SWALLOW EVERYTHING.

WHILST THEY WERE AT IT A STEAMBOAT LANDED...

IN ABOUT TWO MINUTES UP COMES A CROWD A-WHOOPING AND YELLING AND LAUGHING AND CARRYING ON, AND SINGING OUT:

HERE'S YOUR OPPOSITION LINE! HERE'S YOUR TWO SETS O' HEIRS TO OLD PETER WILKS - AND YOU PAYS YOUR MONEY AND YOU TAKES YOUR CHOICE!

THEY WAS FETCHING A VERY NICE-LOOKING OLD GENTLEMAN ALONG, AND A NICE-LOOKING YOUNGER ONE, WITH HIS RIGHT ARM IN A SLING.

BUT I DIDN'T SEE NO JOKE ABOUT IT, AND I JUDGED IT WOULD STRAIN THE DUKE AND THE KING SOME TO SEE ANY. I RECKONED THEY'D TURN PALE. BUT NO, NARY A PALE DID THEY TURN.

AND, MY SOULS, HOW THE PEOPLE YELLED AND LAUGHED, AND KEPT IT UP.

THE KING, HE JUST GAZED AND GAZED DOWN SORROWFUL ON THEM NEW-COMERS LIKE IT GIVE HIM THE STOMACH-ACHE IN HIS VERY HEART TO THINK THERE COULD BE SUCH FRAUDS AND RASCALS IN THE WORLD.

OH, HE DONE IT ADMIRABLE.

WE'LL TAKE THESE FELLOWS TO THE TAVERN AND AFFRONT THEM WITH T'OTHER COUPLE, AND I RECKON WE'LL FIND OUT SOMETHING BEFORE WE GET THROUGH.

I DON'T WISH TO BE TOO HARD ON THESE TWO MEN, BUT I THINK THEY'RE FRAUDS.

IF THESE MEN AIN'T FRAUDS, THEY WON'T OBJECT TO SENDING FOR THAT MONEY AND LETTING US KEEP IT TILL THEY PROVE THEY'RE ALL RIGHT - AIN'T THAT SO?

GENTLEMEN, I WISH THE MONEY WAS THERE, BUT THE NIGGERS STOLE IT THE VERY NEXT MORNIN' AFTER I HAD WENT DOWN STAIRS.

WHEN I SOLD 'EM I HADN'T MISSED THE MONEY YIT, SO THEY GOT CLEAN AWAY WITH IT.

MY SERVANT HERE K'N TELL YOU 'BOUT IT, GENTLEMEN.

ONE MAN ASKED ME IF I SEE THE NIGGERS STEAL IT. I SAID NO, BUT I SEE THEM SNEAKING OUT OF THE ROOM AND HUSTLING AWAY.

WELL, THEN THEY SAILED IN ON THE GENERAL INVESTIGATION, AND THERE WE HAD IT, UP AND DOWN, HOUR IN, HOUR OUT.

BY AND BY THEY HAD ME UP TO TELL WHAT I KNOWED.

STAAARE

I BEGUN TO TELL ABOUT SHEFFIELD, AND HOW WE LIVED THERE, AND ALL ABOUT THE ENGLISH WILKSES, AND SO ON; BUT I DIDN'T GET PRETTY FUR TILL THE DOCTOR BEGUN TO LAUGH.

THE KING HE GIVE ME A LEFT-HANDED LOOK OUT OF THE CORNER OF HIS EYE, AND SO I KNOWED ENOUGH TO TALK ON THE RIGHT SIDE.

HE TOLD ME TO SET DOWN, AS HE RECKONED I WARN'T USED TO LYING AND WANTED PRACTICE.

I DIDN'T CARE NOTHING FOR THE COMPLIMENT, BUT I WAS GLAD TO BE LET OFF, ANYWAY.

GULP

IT *WAS* THE WORST MIXED-UP THING YOU EVER SEE.

ANYBODY BUT A LOT OF PREJUDICED CHUCKLEHEADS WOULD A *SEEN* THAT THE OLD GENTLEMAN WAS SPINNING TRUTH AND T'OTHER ONE LIES.

MURMUR

MURMUR

FINALLY THEY GOT SOME PAPER AND A PEN, AND THE KING HE SET DOWN AND SCRAWLED OFF SOMETHING.

THE NEW OLD GENTLEMAN WROTE SOMETHING, BUT NOBODY COULDN'T READ IT.

SCRIT SCRIT

SCRIT SCRIT

HE SAID ANYBODY COULD SEE THAT THE KING DIDN'T WRITE THEM – BUT THE NEW OLD MAN, THE SCRATCHES HE MAKES AIN'T PROPERLY *WRITING* AT ALL!

THEN THE LAWYER SNAKED A LOT OF OLD LETTERS FROM HARVEY WILKS OUT OF HIS POCKET AND EXAMINED THE WRITING.

BUT HE CAN'T WRITE WITH HIS LEFT HAND...

IF YOU PLEASE, LET ME EXPLAIN. NOBODY CAN READ MY HAND BUT MY BROTHER THERE – SO HE COPIES FOR ME. IT'S *HIS* HAND YOU'VE GOT THERE, NOT MINE.

WELL! THAT *WAS* A STATE OF THINGS.

PERHAPS THIS GENTLEMAN CAN TELL ME WHAT WAS TATTOOED ON PETER WILKS' BREAST?

I'VE THOUGHT OF SOMETHING.

SAYS I TO MYSELF, NOW HE'LL THROW UP THE SPONGE – THERE AIN'T NO MORE USE. WELL, DID HE? A BODY CAN'T HARDLY BELIEVE IT, BUT HE DIDN'T.

MF! IT'S A VERY TOUGH QUESTION, AIN'T IT! YES, SIR, I K'N TELL YOU WHAT'S TATTOOED ON HIS BREAST. IT'S JEST A SMALL, THIN, BLUE ARROW.

WELL, I NEVER SEE ANYTHING LIKE THAT OLD BLISTER FOR CLEAN OUT-AND-OUT CHEEK.

WHAT YOU WOULD SEE ON HIS BREAST WAS A SMALL DIM P, AND A B, AND A W, WITH DASHES BETWEEN THEM.

BUT THE MEN WHO LAID OUT PETER WILKS FOR BURYING SAID THEY NEVER SEEN ANY MARKS AT ALL.

WELL, EVERYBODY *WAS* IN A STATE OF MIND NOW.

THE WHOLE *BILIN'* OF 'M 'S FRAUDS!

LE'S DUCK 'EM! LE'S DROWN 'EM!

LE'S RIDE 'EM ON A RAIL!

THE DOCTOR HE JUMPS ON THE TABLE AND YELLS:

GENTLEMEN - GENTLEMEN! THERE'S ONE WAY YET - LET'S GO AND DIG UP THE CORPSE AND LOOK.

THEY GRIPPED US ALL, AND MARCHED US RIGHT ALONG.

THERE WARN'T NO GETTING AWAY, YOU KNOW.

HOORAY!

THAT TOOK THEM, AND THEY WAS STARTING RIGHT OFF.

CRCK BOOM

EVERYTHING WAS GOING SO DIFFERENT FROM WHAT I HAD ALLOWED FOR.

THIS WAS THE MOST AWFUL TROUBLE AND MOST DANGERSOME I EVER WAS IN.

I WAS KINDER STUNNED.

THUNK

THAT BIG HUSKY HINES HAD ME TIGHT AND A BODY MIGHT AS WELL TRY TO GIVE GOLIAR THE SLIP.

STEAD OF BEING FIXED SO I COULD HAVE MARY JANE AT MY BACK TO SAVE ME, HERE WAS NOTHING IN THE WORLD BETWIXT ME AND SUDDEN DEATH BUT JUST THEM TATTOO-MARKS.

IF THEY DIDN'T FIND THEM –

EH?

IF WE DON'T FIND THEM MARKS WE 'LL LYNCH THE WHOLE GANG!

I COULDN'T BEAR TO THINK ABOUT IT; AND YET, SOMEHOW, I COULDN'T THINK ABOUT NOTHING ELSE.

BY THE LIVING JINGO!

HERE'S THE BAG OF GOLD ON HIS BREAST!

I FAIRLY FLEW.

HEY!

WHAT?!

...

ZOOM

SLIP

SURE AS YOU ARE BORN I DID CLIP IT ALONG!

WHEN I STRUCK THE TOWN I SEE THERE WARN'T NOBODY OUT IN THE STORM, SO I NEVER HUNTED FOR NO BACK STREETS, BUT HUMPED IT STRAIGHT THROUGH THE MAIN ONE.

HUF HUF HUF

THE FIRST TIME THE LIGHTNING SHOWED ME A BOAT THAT WASN'T CHAINED I SNATCHED IT AND SHOVED.

HUCK?

LET'S GO...!

GLORY BE TO GOODNESS, WE'RE SHUT OF THEM!

OUT WITH YOU, JIM, AND SET HER LOOSE!

275

WHEEE

LOOOM

I FORGOT HE WAS OLD KING LEAR AND A DROWNDED A-RAB ALL IN ONE - THAT MOST SCARED THE LIVERS AND LIGHTS OUT OF ME!

WAAAAA -!!

NOT NOW; HAVE IT FOR BREAKFAST, HAVE IT FOR BREAKFAST! CUT LOOSE AND LET HER SLIDE!

JIM HE WAS GOING TO HUG ME AND BLESS ME, BUT...

WHAT...?

SPLASH SPLASH SPLASH

SO IN TWO SECONDS AWAY WE WENT A-SLIDING DOWN THE RIVER.

IT WAS THE KING AND THE DUKE.

I WILTED RIGHT DOWN ON TO THE PLANKS THEN, AND GIVE UP; AND IT WAS ALL I COULD DO TO KEEP FROM CRYING.

YANK

TRYIN' TO GIVE US THE SLIP, WAS YE, YOU PUP! TIRED OF OUR COMPANY, HEY?

NO, YOUR MAJESTY, WE WARN'T – PLEASE DON'T, YOUR MAJESTY!

I WAS AFEARD YOU AND THE DUKE WASN'T ALIVE NOW, AND I WAS AWFUL SORRY, AND SO WAS JIM, AND WAS AWFUL GLAD WHEN WE SEE YOU COMING; YOU MAY ASK JIM IF I DIDN'T.

LEGGO THE BOY, YOU OLD IDIOT! WOULD YOU A DONE ANY DIFFERENT? DID YOU INQUIRE AROUND FOR HIM WHEN YOU GOT LOOSE? I DON'T REMEMBER IT.

SIGH

CHAPTER XXX

---? ---!

---!

THAT MADE ME SQUIRM!

THEY WAS STILL A MINUTE – THINKING; THEN THEY BOTH GOT TO HINTING AROUND HOW THEY KNEW WHO HAD STOLE THE MONEY.

BUT THE KING KIND OF RUFFLES UP, AND TALKS ALL SARCASTIC, AND THEN THE DUKE BRISTLES UP AFTER – THEY BOTH THOUGHT THE OTHER HAD DONE IT!

THE DUKE WENT FOR HIM.

IT'S A LIE!

TAKE Y'R HANDS OFF! – LEGGO MY THROAT! – I TAKE IT ALL BACK!

THE KING OWNED UP AFTER HE STARTED TO GURGLE, AND I WAS VERY GLAD TO HEAR HIM SAY IT.

WHEN THEY GOT TO SNORING WE HAD A LONG GABBLE, AND I TOLD JIM EVERYTHING.

THE KING SNEAKED INTO THE WIGWAM AND TOOK TO HIS BOTTLE FOR COMFORT, AND BEFORE LONG THE DUKE TACKLED HIS BOTTLE.

IN ABOUT A HALF AN HOUR THEY WAS AS THICK AS THIEVES AGAIN, A-SNORING IN EACH OTHER'S ARMS.

WE JUDGED THEY WAS STUDYING UP SOME KIND OF WORSE DEVILTRY THAN EVER.

CHAPTER XXXI

SO AT LAST THEY GOT JUST ABOUT DEAD BROKE, DREADFUL BLUE AND DESPERATE, AND BEGUN TO LAY THEIR HEADS TOGETHER AND TALK LOW AND CONFIDENTIAL.

WE DASN'T STOP AGAIN AT ANY TOWN FOR DAYS AND DAYS, UNTIL THE FRAUDS RECKONED THEY WERE OUT OF DANGER.

THEY TACKLED MISSIONARYING, AND MESMERIZING, AND DOCTORING, AND TELLING FORTUNES, AND A LITTLE OF EVERYTHING; BUT THEY COULDN'T SEEM TO HAVE NO LUCK.

MURMUR   MURMUR

A FEW DAYS LATER

EARLY ONE MORNING WE HID THE RAFT ABOUT TWO MILE BELOW A SHABBY VILLAGE NAMED PIKESVILLE.

JIM AND ME GOT UNEASY. WE DIDN'T LIKE THE LOOK OF IT.

HE SAID IF HE WARN'T BACK BY MIDDAY THE DUKE AND ME WOULD KNOW IT WAS ALL RIGHT, AND WE WAS TO COME ALONG.

THE KING HE WENT ASHORE AND TOLD US ALL TO STAY HID WHILST HE WENT UP TO TOWN AND SMELT AROUND TO SEE IF ANYBODY HAD GOT ANY WIND OF THE ROYAL NONESUCH THERE YET.

SO ME AND THE DUKE WENT UP TO THE VILLAGE AT MIDDAY AND BY AND BY WE FOUND THE KING IN THE BACK ROOM OF A LITTLE LOW DOGGERY, VERY TIGHT.

THE DUKE HE BEGUN TO ABUSE HIM FOR AN OLD FOOL, AND THE KING BEGUN TO SASS BACK.

I GOT DOWN THERE ALL OUT OF BREATH BUT LOADED UP WITH JOY.

SET HER LOOSE, JIM!

I SPUN DOWN THE RIVER ROAD LIKE A DEER, FOR I SEE OUR CHANCE.

THE MINUTE THEY WAS FAIRLY AT IT I LIT OUT AND SHOOK THE REEFS OUT OF MY HIND LEGS.

HEH HEH

BUT THERE WARN'T NO ANSWER.

NOBODY COME OUT OF THE WIGWAM. JIM WAS GONE!

I RUN THIS WAY AND THAT IN THE WOODS, WHOOPING AND SCREECHING.

HEY!

THUMP THUMP

I SET UP A SHOUT - AND THEN ANOTHER - AND THEN ANOTHER ONE.

BUT I COULDN'T SET STILL LONG. PRETTY SOON I WENT OUT ON THE ROAD, TRYING TO THINK WHAT I BETTER DO.

I RUN ACROSS A BOY WALKING.

I ASKED HIM IF HE'D SEEN A STRANGE NIGGER DRESSED SO AND SO. AND HE SAYS:

YES.

WHERE-ABOUTS?

DOWN TO SILAS PHELPS' PLACE, TWO MILE BELOW HERE.

YOU BET I AIN'T!

HE'S A RUNAWAY NIGGER, AND THEY'VE GOT HIM. WAS YOU LOOKING FOR HIM?

GYAAAARRR

I RUN ACROSS HIM IN THE WOODS ABOUT AN HOUR OR TWO AGO,

AND HE SAID IF I HOLLERED HE'D CUT MY LIVERS OUT — AND TOLD ME TO LAY DOWN AND STAY WHERE I WAS; AND I DONE IT.

BEEN THERE EVER SINCE; AFEARD TO COME OUT.

WELL, YOU NEEDN'T BE AFEARD NO MORE, BECUZ THEY'VE GOT HIM.

WHO NAILED HIM?

WELL, I RECKON! THERE'S TWO HUNDERD DOLLARS REWARD ON HIM.

IT'S A GOOD JOB THEY GOT HIM.

282

IT WAS AN OLD FELLOW – A STRANGER – AND HE SOLD OUT HIS CHANCE IN HIM FOR FORTY DOLLARS.

THINK O' THAT, NOW!

SAID IT'S BECUZ HE'S GOT TO GO UP THE RIVER AN CAN'T WAIT.

AFTER ALL WE DONE FOR THEM SCOUNDRELS, HERE IT'S ALL COME TO NOTHING.

MAYBE THERE'S SOMETHING AIN'T STRAIGHT ABOUT IT?

BUT IT IS, THOUGH – STRAIGHT AS A STRING.

I WENT TO THE RAFT, AND SET DOWN IN THE WIGWAM TO THINK.

BECAUSE THEY HAD THE HEART TO SERVE JIM SUCH A TRICK AS THAT, AND MAKE HIM A SLAVE AGAIN ALL HIS LIFE.

AND AMONGST STRANGERS, TOO, FOR FORTY DIRTY DOLLARS.

IT WOULD BE A THOUSAND TIMES BETTER FOR JIM TO BE A SLAVE AT HOME WHERE HIS FAMILY WAS, AS LONG AS HE'D GOT TO BE A SLAVE.

THUMP

SO I'D BETTER WRITE A LETTER TO TOM SAWYER AND TELL HIM TO TELL MISS WATSON WHERE HE WAS.

AND IF SHE DIDN'T, EVERYBODY NATURALLY DESPISES AN UNGRATEFUL NIGGER, AND THEY'D MAKE JIM FEEL IT ALL THE TIME, AND SO HE'D FEEL ORNERY AND DISGRACED.

BUT SHE'D BE MAD AND DISGUSTED AT HIS RASCALITY AND UNGRATEFULNESS FOR LEAVING HER...

SHE'D SELL HIM STRAIGHT DOWN THE RIVER AGAIN.

WHUMP

284

IF I WAS EVER TO SEE ANYBODY FROM THAT TOWN AGAIN I'D BE READY TO GET DOWN AND LICK HIS BOOTS FOR SHAME.

AND THEN THINK OF *ME*!

IT WOULD GET ALL AROUND THAT HUCK FINN HELPED A NIGGER TO GET HIS FREEDOM.

THINKS AS LONG AS HE CAN HIDE IT, IT AIN'T NO DISGRACE. THAT WAS MY FIX EXACTLY.

THAT'S JUST THE WAY: A PERSON DOES A LOW-DOWN THING, AND THEN HE DON'T WANT TO TAKE NO CONSEQUENCES OF IT.

THE MORE MY CONSCIENCE WENT TO GRINDING ME.

THE MORE I STUDIED ABOUT THIS,

AND AT LAST, IT HIT ME ALL OF A SUDDEN THAT HERE WAS THE PLAIN HAND OF PROVIDENCE SLAPPING ME IN THE FACE AND LETTING ME KNOW MY WICKEDNESS WAS BEING WATCHED ALL THE TIME FROM UP THERE IN HEAVEN,

WHILST I WAS STEALING A POOR OLD WOMAN'S NIGGER THAT HADN'T EVER DONE ME NO HARM.

I MOST DROPPED IN MY TRACKS I WAS SO SCARED.

THERE'S ONE THAT'S ALWAYS ON THE LOOKOUT, AND AIN'T A-GOING TO ALLOW NO SUCH MISERABLE DOINGS TO GO ONLY JUST SO FUR AND NO FURTHER.

IT MADE ME SHIVER.

BUT SOMETHING INSIDE OF ME KEPT SAYING, "THERE WAS THE SUNDAY-SCHOOL, YOU COULD A GONE TO IT; AND IF YOU'D A DONE IT THEY'D A LEARNT YOU THERE THAT PEOPLE THAT ACTS AS I'D BEEN ACTING ABOUT THAT NIGGER GOES TO EVERLASTING FIRE."

I ABOUT MADE UP MY MIND TO PRAY, AND SEE IF I COULDN'T TRY TO QUIT BEING THE KIND OF A BOY I WAS AND BE BETTER.

SO I KNEELED DOWN. BUT THE WORDS WOULDN'T COME.

SHUDDER

WHY WOULDN'T THEY?

IT WARN'T NO USE TO TRY AND HIDE IT FROM HIM. NOR FROM ME, NEITHER.

I KNOWED VERY WELL WHY THEY WOULDN'T COME.

287

IT WAS BECAUSE MY HEART WARN'T RIGHT; IT WAS BECAUSE I WARN'T SQUARE; IT WAS BECAUSE I WAS PLAYING DOUBLE.

I WAS LETTING ON TO GIVE UP SIN, BUT AWAY INSIDE OF ME I WAS HOLDING ON TO THE BIGGEST ONE OF ALL.

AT LAST I HAD AN IDEA.

YOU CAN'T PRAY A LIE – I FOUND THAT OUT.

I'LL GO AND WRITE THE LETTER – AND THEN SEE IF I CAN PRAY.

Miss Watson,

Your runaway nigger Jim is down here two mile below Pikesville, and Mr. Phelps has got him and he will give him up for the reward if you send.

HUCK FINN.

I FELT GOOD.

ALL WASHED CLEAN OF SIN FOR THE FIRST TIME I HAD EVER FELT SO IN MY LIFE.

I KNOWED I COULD PRAY NOW.

...

...

...

TWITCH?

...

WUB

...

HUCK; YOU'S DE BEST' FREN' JIM'S EVER HAD; EN YOU'S DE ONLY FREN' OLE JIM'S GOT NOW.

ALL RIGHT, THEN.

I'LL GO TO HELL.

RIIIIIP—

AND FOR A STARTER I WOULD GO TO WORK AND STEAL JIM OUT OF SLAVERY AGAIN.

IT WAS AWFUL THOUGHTS AND AWFUL WORDS, BUT THEY WAS SAID. AND I LET THEM STAY SAID; AND NEVER THOUGHT NO MORE ABOUT REFORMING.

AND IF I COULD THINK UP ANYTHING WORSE, I WOULD DO THAT, TOO.

BECAUSE AS LONG AS I WAS IN, AND IN FOR GOOD, I MIGHT AS WELL GO THE WHOLE HOG.

I SHOVED THE WHOLE THING OUT OF MY HEAD, AND SAID I WOULD TAKE UP WICKEDNESS AGAIN, WHICH WAS IN MY LINE, BEING BRUNG UP TO IT, AND THE OTHER WARN'T.

THEN I SET TO THINKING OVER HOW TO GET AT IT, AND TURNED OVER SOME CONSIDERABLE MANY WAYS IN MY MIND.

I TOOK THE BEARINGS OF A WOODY ISLAND THAT WAS DOWN THE RIVER A PIECE.

I CREPT OUT WITH MY RAFT AND WENT FOR IT, AND HID IT THERE.

I SLEPT THE NIGHT THROUGH, AND GOT UP BEFORE IT WAS LIGHT, AND CLEARED FOR SHORE.

WELL, THE VERY FIRST MAN I SEE WHEN I GOT THERE WAS THE DUKE.

WHERE'S THE RAFT? – GOT HER IN A GOOD PLACE?

HEL-LO! WHERE'D YOU COME FROM?

?

THEY HAVE THE CHEEK, THEM FRAUDS!

BILLS FOR THE ROYAL NONESUCH – THREE-NIGHT PERFORMANCE – LIKE THAT OTHER TIME.

WHAT WAS YOUR IDEA FOR ASKING ME?

WHY, THAT'S JUST WHAT I WAS GOING TO ASK YOUR GRACE.

I GOT THERE AND SEE IT WAS GONE! I SAYS TO MYSELF, 'THEY'VE GOT INTO TROUBLE AND HAD TO LEAVE!"

WHAT *DID* BECOME OF THE RAFT, THEN? – AND JIM – POOR JIM!

AND I SAYS TO MYSELF, "AND NOW I'M IN A STRANGE COUNTRY, AND AIN'T GOT NO PROPERTY NO MORE, NOR NOTHING, AND NO WAY TO MAKE MY LIVING!"

THAT IS, WHAT'S BECOME OF THE RAFT.

HEH

BLAMED IF I KNOW –

WHEN I GOT HIM HOME LATE LAST NIGHT AND FOUND THE RAFT GONE, WE SAID, 'THAT LITTLE RASCAL HAS STOLE OUR RAFT AND SHOOK US, AND RUN OFF DOWN THE RIVER.'

THAT OLD FOOL HAD MADE A TRADE AND GOT FORTY DOLLARS, AND WHEN WE FOUND HIM IN THE DOGGERY HE'D GAMBLED IT ALL AWAY!

WHAAAAAA-?

WE NEVER THOUGHT OF THAT.

I WOULDN'T SHAKE MY *NIGGER,* WOULD I? – THE ONLY NIGGER I HAD IN THE WORLD, AND THE ONLY PROPERTY.

DO YOU RECKON THAT NIGGER WOULD BLOW ON US?

FACT IS, I RECKON WE'D COME TO CONSIDER HIM OUR NIGGER.

...

HOW CAN HE BLOW? HAIN'T HE RUN OFF?

WE'D SKIN HIM IF HE DONE THAT!

WHY, HE WAS MY NIGGER, AND THAT WAS MY MONEY!

SOLD HIM?

NO! THAT OLD FOOL SOLD HIM, AND NEVER DIVIDED WITH ME, AND THE MONEY'S GONE.

LOOKY HERE.

WELL, YOU CAN'T GET YOUR NIGGER, THAT'S ALL - SO DRY UP YOUR BLUBBERING.

WHERE IS HE? - I WANT MY NIGGER.

AAAGH-

NAB

GRAB

!

DO YOU THINK *YOU'D* VENTURE TO BLOW ON US? BLAMED IF I THINK I'D TRUST YOU.

FLUT

I'LL TELL YOU SOME-THING.

I GOT TO TURN OUT AND FIND MY NIGGER.

WHY, IF YOU *WAS* TO BLOW ON US -

WE GOT TO BE HERE THREE DAYS. IF YOU'LL PROMISE YOU WON'T BLOW, AND WON'T LET THE NIGGER BLOW, I'LL TELL YOU WHERE TO FIND HIM.

I DON'T WANT TO BLOW ON NOBODY; AND I AIN'T GOT NO TIME TO BLOW, NOHOW.

I PROMISE!

A FARMER BY THE NAME OF SILAS PH –

...

THE MAN THAT BOUGHT HIM IS NAMED ABRAM FOSTER – ABRAM G. FOSTER – AND HE LIVES FORTY MILE BACK HERE IN THE COUNTRY, ON THE ROAD TO LAFAYETTE.

DON'T YOU LOSE ANY TIME ABOUT IT.

AND I'LL START THIS VERY AFTERNOON!

HE DON'T TRUST ME; HE WANTS TO MAKE SURE OF HAVING ME OUT OF THE WAY THE WHOLE THREE DAYS.

ALL RIGHT, I CAN WALK IT IN THREE DAYS.

JUST KEEP A TIGHT TONGUE IN YOUR HEAD AND MOVE RIGHT ALONG.

THEN YOU WON'T GET INTO TROUBLE WITH US, D'YE HEAR?

I DIDN'T WANT NO TROUBLE WITH THEIR KIND.

THAT WAS THE ORDER I WANTED, AND THAT WAS THE ONE I PLAYED FOR. I WANTED TO BE LEFT FREE TO WORK MY PLANS.

IT WAS ALL STILL AND SUNDAY-LIKE, AND HOT AND SUNSHINY.

THERE WAS THEM KIND OF FAINT DRONINGS OF BUGS AND FLIES IN THE AIR THAT MAKES IT SEEM SO LONESOME AND LIKE EVERYBODY'S DEAD AND GONE.

CHAPTER XXXII

LIKE SPIRITS WHISPERING -

THOMP!

FEELS LIKE THOSE SPIRITS'RE TALKING ABOUT ME.

PHELPS FARM

THEN I KNOWED FOR CERTAIN I WISHED I WAS DEAD - FOR THAT *IS* THE LONESOMEST SOUND IN THE WHOLE WORLD.

WHEN I GOT A LITTLE WAYS I HEARD THE DIM HUM OF A SPINNING-WHEEL WAILING ALONG UP AND SINKING ALONG DOWN AGAIN.

ARF!

WOOF!

I WENT RIGHT ALONG, NOT FIXING UP ANY PARTICULAR PLAN.

I'D JUST TRUST TO PROVIDENCE TO PUT THE RIGHT WORDS IN MY MOUTH WHEN THE TIME COME.

WOOF!

WOOF!

BEGONE *YOU* TIGE! YOU SPOT! BEGONE SAH!

IT'S *YOU*, AT LAST! - AIN'T IT?

NOW I CAN HAVE A *GOOD* LOOK AT YOU.

YES'M.

I'M SO GLAD TO SEE YOU! DEAR, DEAR, IT DOES SEEM LIKE I COULD EAT YOU UP!

YOU DON'T LOOK AS MUCH LIKE YOUR MOTHER AS I RECKONED YOU WOULD; BUT LAW SAKES, I DON'T CARE FOR THAT.

WE BEEN EXPECTING YOU A COUPLE OF DAYS AND MORE. WHAT KEP' YOU? – BOAT GET AGROUND?

I DON'T RIGHTLY KNOW WHAT TO SAY...

LIZE, HURRY UP AND GET HIM A HOT BREAKFAST RIGHT AWAY –

– OR DID YOU GET YOUR BREAKFAST ON THE BOAT?

YES'M.

I GOT IT ON THE BOAT.

YES'M – SHE –

DON'T SAY YES'M – SAY AUNT SALLY.

I WAS GETTING SO UNEASY I COULDN'T LISTEN GOOD.

I WANTED TO GET THE CHILDREN OUT TO ONE SIDE AND PUMP THEM A LITTLE, AND FIND OUT WHO I WAS.

BUT I COULDN'T GET NO SHOW, MRS. PHELPS KEPT IT UP AND RUN ON SO.

I DIDN'T RIGHTLY KNOW WHAT TO SAY, AND SOON SHE MADE THE COLD CHILLS STREAK ALL DOWN MY BACK, BECAUSE SHE STARTS ASKING ABOUT HER RELATIONS, AND I DON'T RIGHTLY KNOW WHO THEY'D BE!

BUT JUST THEN SHE HUSTLED ME IN BEHIND THE BED INSTEAD.

WELL, I WAS UP A STUMP, AND UP IT GOOD.

HERE HE COMES! DON'T YOU LET ON YOU'RE HERE.

HERE'S ANOTHER PLACE WHERE I GOT TO RESK THE TRUTH...

CHILDREN, DON'T YOU SAY A WORD.

SHH

HAS HE COME?

I SEE I WAS IN A FIX NOW. BUT THERE WARN'T NOTHING TO DO BUT JUST HOLD STILL, AND TRY AND BE READY TO STAND FROM UNDER WHEN THE LIGHTNING STRUCK.

SIGH

NO, AND I MUST SAY IT MAKES ME DREADFUL UNEASY.

UNEASY! I'M READY TO GO DISTRACTED!

HE MUST A COME; AND YOU'VE MISSED HIM ALONG THE ROAD.

SALLY, IT'S TERRIBLE – JUST TERRIBLE – SOMETHING'S HAPPENED TO THE BOAT, SURE!

?

WHY, SILAS! LOOK YONDER! AIN'T THAT SOMEBODY COMING?

303

...

I DON'T SEE –

WHY, WHO'S THAT?

WHO DO YOU RECKON 'T IS?

I HAIN'T NO IDEA. WHO IS IT?

HA HA!

IT'S TOM SAWYER!

!

BY JINGS, I MOST SLUMPED THROUGH THE FLOOR!

THEY WAS SO JOYFUL, AND THEY FROZE TO ME FOR TWO HOURS AND FIRED OFF QUESTIONS ABOUT SID, AND MARY, AND THE REST OF THE TRIBE.

WHOMP

IT WAS LIKE BEING BORN AGAIN, I WAS SO GLAD TO FIND OUT WHO I WAS.

NOW I WAS FEELING PRETTY COMFORTABLE ALL DOWN ONE SIDE, AND PRETTY UNCOMFORTABLE ALL UP THE OTHER.

BEING TOM SAWYER WAS EASY AND COMFORTABLE, BUT S'POSE TOM SAWYER COMES DOWN ON THE NEXT BOAT? AND S'POSE HE STEPS IN HERE ANY MINUTE, AND SINGS OUT MY NAME BEFORE I CAN THROW HIM A WINK TO KEEP QUIET?

WELL, I COULDN'T *HAVE* IT THAT WAY.

CHAPTER XXXIII

SO I TOLD THE FOLKS I RECKONED I WOULD GO UP TO THE TOWN AND FETCH DOWN MY BAGGAGE, AND I STARTED FOR TOWN, IN THE WAGON.

WHEN I WAS HALF-WAY I SEE A WAGON COMING.

TAK
TAK
TAK

HOLD ON!

SURE ENOUGH, IT WAS TOM SAWYER.

... HUCK?

I HAIN'T COME BACK - I HAIN'T BEEN GONE.

SHNER

SHNER

I HAIN'T EVER DONE YOU NO HARM. YOU KNOW THAT. SO, THEN, WHAT YOU WANT TO COME BACK AND HA'NT ME FOR?

DON'T YOU PLAY NOTHING ON ME, BECAUSE I WOULDN'T ON YOU. HONEST INJUN, YOU AIN'T A GHOST?

HONEST INJUN, I AIN'T.

LOOKY HERE, WARN'T YOU EVER MURDERED AT ALL?

YOU COME IN HERE AND FEEL OF ME IF YOU DON'T BELIEVE ME.

SO HE DONE IT.

PAT

PAT

PAT

PAT

GRAB

WELL?

...

BY AND BY I TOLD HIM THE KIND OF A FIX I WAS IN, AND WHAT DID HE RECKON WE BETTER DO?

WHAM

HUCK -!!

AAGH!

ALL RIGHT; BUT WAIT A MINUTE. THERE'S ONE MORE THING -

IT'S ALL RIGHT; I'VE GOT IT. I'LL GET THERE A QUARTER OR A HALF AN HOUR AFTER YOU.

A THING THAT NOBODY DON'T KNOW BUT ME.

WHAT IS IT?

THERE'S A NIGGER HERE THAT I'M A-TRYING TO STEAL OUT OF SLAVERY, AND HIS NAME IS JIM - OLD MISS WATSON'S JIM.

WHAT! WHY, JIM IS -

BUT WHAT IF IT IS? I'M LOW DOWN; AND I'M A-GOING TO STEAL HIM.

I KNOW WHAT YOU'LL SAY. YOU'LL SAY IT'S DIRTY, LOW-DOWN BUSINESS.

WHAT!?

AND I WANT YOU KEEP MUM AND NOT LET ON. WILL YOU?

I'LL HELP YOU!

I'LL HELP YOU STEAL HIM!

TOM SAWYER A NIGGER-STEALER!

I'M BOUND TO SAY TOM SAWYER FELL CONSIDERABLE IN MY ESTIMATION.

OH, SHUCKS! YOU'RE JOKING.

I AIN'T JOKING, EITHER.

WELL, THEN.

HA HA HA HA

TOM HE ARRIVED IN ABOUT HALF AN HOUR, AND TOLD EVERYONE THAT HE WAS HIS BROTHER SID, COME AT THE LAST MINUTE.

AUNT SALLY HUGGED HIM AND KISSED HIM OVER AND OVER AGAIN, AND THEN TURNED HIM OVER TO THE OLD MAN, AND HE TOOK WHAT WAS LEFT.

MMMMMM

PHELPS' HOUSE

PA, MAYN'T TOM AND SID AND ME GO TO THE SHOW?

AT SUPPER, THAT NIGHT

NO, I RECKON THERE AIN'T GOING TO BE ANY; AND YOU COULDN'T GO IF THERE WAS.

SO THERE IT WAS! - BUT I COULDN'T HELP IT.

THE RUNAWAY NIGGER TOLD BURTON AND ME ALL ABOUT THAT SCANDALOUS SHOW, AND BURTON SAID HE WOULD TELL THE PEOPLE;

SO I RECKON THEY'VE DROVE THE OWDACIOUS LOAFERS OUT OF TOWN BEFORE THIS TIME.

AS WE STRUCK THE TOWN HERE COMES A RAGING RUSH OF PEOPLE WITH TORCHES, AND AN AWFUL WHOOPING AND YELLING.

THEN WE CLUMB OUT OF THE WINDOW AND SHOVED FOR THE TOWN.

TAK TAK TAK TAK

TOM AND ME BID GOOD-NIGHT AND WENT UP TO BED RIGHT AFTER SUPPER.

WE JUMPED TO ONE SIDE TO LET THEM GO BY.

BAR

IT WAS A DREADFUL THING TO SEE. HUMAN BEINGS *CAN* BE AWFUL CRUEL TO ONE ANOTHER.

RAAAAAAR

AS THEY WENT BY I SEE THEY HAD THE KING AND THE DUKE ASTRADDLE OF A RAIL — THEY WAS ALL OVER TAR AND FEATHERS, AND DIDN'T LOOK LIKE NOTHING IN THE WORLD THAT WAS HUMAN.

BOOoo

SOLD

GET 'EM

CHAPTER XXXIV

LOOKY HERE, HUCK.

...

I BET I KNOW WHERE JIM IS.

YES. I THOUGHT THE VITTLES WAS FOR A DOG.

WELL, THEY WASN'T.

IN THAT HUT DOWN BY THE ASH-HOPPER. WHEN WE WAS AT DINNER, DIDN'T YOU SEE A NIGGER MAN GO IN THERE WITH SOME VITTLES?

NO! WHERE?

THE NIGGER UNLOCKED THE PADLOCK WHEN HE WENT IN, AND HE LOCKED IT AGAIN WHEN HE CAME OUT. THAT SHOWS PRISONER.

IT AIN'T LIKELY THERE'S TWO PRISONERS ON SUCH A LITTLE PLANTATION.

WHAT A HEAD FOR A BOY TO HAVE!

WE WENT TO THINKING OUT OUR PLANS.

NOW YOU WORK YOUR MIND, AND STUDY OUT A PLAN TO STEAL JIM, AND I WILL STUDY OUT ONE, TOO; AND WE'LL TAKE THE ONE WE LIKE THE BEST.

YES.

READY?

ALL RIGHT – BRING IT OUT.

DING!

THE FIRST DARK NIGHT THAT COMES WE CAN STEAL THE KEY OUT OF THE OLD MAN'S BRITCHES AFTER HE GOES TO BED.

WHOOP!

THEN WE CAN SHOVE OFF DOWN THE RIVER ON THE RAFT WITH JIM.

HIDING DAYTIMES AND RUNNING NIGHTS, THE WAY ME AND JIM USED TO DO BEFORE. WOULDN'T THAT PLAN WORK?

NOW I'VE GOT MY PLAN READY...

WORK? WHY, CERT'NLY IT WOULD WORK. BUT IT'S TOO BLAME' SIMPLE; THERE AIN'T NOTHING TO IT.

WHAT'S THE GOOD OF A PLAN THAT AIN'T NO MORE TROUBLE THAN THAT?

...

...

~~~

YOUR PLAN'S WORTH FIFTEEN OF MINE FOR STYLE, AND IT'LL MAYBE GET US ALL KILLED BESIDES!

HA HA!

WELL, ONE THING'S DEAD SURE:

TOM SAWYER'S IN EARNEST, AND IS ACTULY GOING TO HELP STEAL THAT NIGGER OUT OF SLAVERY.

THAT WAS THE THING THAT WAS TOO MANY FOR ME. HERE WAS A BOY THAT WAS RESPECTABLE AND WELL BRUNG UP; AND YET HERE HE WAS, WITHOUT ANY MORE PRIDE, OR RIGHTNESS, OR FEELING, THAN TO STOOP TO THIS BUSINESS, AND MAKE HIMSELF A SHAME, AND HIS FAMILY A SHAME, BEFORE EVERYBODY. I COULDN'T UNDERSTAND IT NO WAY AT ALL.

IT WAS OUTRAGEOUS, AND I KNOWED I OUGHT TO JUST BE HIS TRUE FRIEND, AND LET HIM QUIT THE THING RIGHT WHERE HE WAS AND SAVE HIMSELF.

YOU HUSH, HUCK.

SAY, TOM –

317

YES.

DON'T YOU RECKON I KNOW WHAT I'M ABOUT? DON'T I GENERLY KNOW WHAT I'M ABOUT?

WELL, THEN.

YES.

DIDN'T I SAY I WAS GOING TO HELP STEAL THE NIGGER?

THA'S ALL HE SAID, AND THAT'S ALL I SAID.

IF HE WAS BOUND TO HAVE IT SO, I COULDN'T HELP IT.

HERE'S THE TICKET. WE'LL MAKE A HOLE'S BIG ENOUGH FOR JIM TO GET THROUGH IF WE WRENCH OFF THIS BOARD.

IT'S AS SIMPLE AS TIT-TAT-TOE. I *HOPE* WE CAN FIND A WAY THAT'S A LITTLE MORE COMPLICATED THAN *THAT*, HUCK FINN.

BUT I BET WE CAN FIND A WAY THAT'S TWICE AS LONG.

WELL, THEN, HOW 'LL IT DO TO SAW HIM OUT, THE WAY I DONE BEFORE I WAS MURDERED THAT TIME?

THAT'S MORE LIKE.

319

!

LET'S TALK TO HIM.

UH...

THERE'S NAT WITH THE VITTLES.

HEY! NAT!

IF WE CAN MAKE FRIENDS WITH THE NIGGER WHO FEEDS JIM...

THIS NIGGER HAD A GOOD-NATURED, CHUCKLE-HEADED FACE.

HIS WOOL WAS ALL TIED UP IN LITTLE BUNCHES WITH THREAD. THAT WAS TO KEEP WITCHES OFF.

THAT WARN'T THE PLAN.

IT'S THE PLAN NOW.

WHAT'S THE VITTLES FOR? GOING TO FEED THE DOGS?

YES, MARS SID, A DOG. CUR'US DOG, TOO. DOES YOU WANT TO GO EN LOOK AT 'IM?

YES.

WELL, DRAT HIM.

!

OHHH WHY, HUCK! EN GOOD LAN'! AIN' DAT MISTO TOM?

WHY, DE GRACIOUS SAKES! DO HE KNOW YOU GENLMEN?

WHY, DIS-YER RUNAWAY NIGGER.

DOES *WHO* KNOW US?

I DON'T RECKON HE DOES; BUT WHAT PUT THAT INTO YOUR HEAD?

WHAT *PUT* IT DAR? DIDN' HE JIS' DIS MINUTE SING OUT LIKE HE KNOWED YOU?

WHAT DO YOU RECKON'S THE MATTER WITH YOU, ANYWAY?

DID *YOU* HEAR ANYBODY SING OUT?

NO, I HAIN'T.

OH, IT'S DE DAD-BLAME' WITCHES, SAH!

NAT, DON'T BE AFRAID. GIVE ME YOUR HAND.

DEY'S AWLUZ AT IT, SAH, EN DEY DO MOS' KILL ME, DEY SK'YERS ME SO.

DID YOU SING OUT?

NO, SAH, I HAIN'T SAID NOTHING, SAH.

BUY SOME MORE THREAD TO TIE UP YOUR WOOL WITH, SO YOU DON'T NEED TO BE AFRAID NO MORE.

THANK YOU, MARS SID.

YOU'RE WELCOME!

...

NOW HERE'S A DIME.

DON'T EVER LET ON TO KNOW US. AND IF YOU HEAR ANY DIGGING GOING ON NIGHTS, IT'S US; WE'RE GOING TO SET YOU FREE.

JIM ONLY HAD TIME TO GRAB US BY THE HAND AND SQUEEZE IT; THEN THE NIGGER COME BACK.

IT MAKES IT SO ROTTEN DIFFICULT TO GET UP A DIFFICULT PLAN.

BLAME IT, THIS WHOLE THING IS JUST AS EASY AND AWKWARD AS IT CAN BE!

CHAPTER XXXV

WHY, ALL YOU GOT TO DO IS TO LIFT UP THE BEDSTEAD AND SLIP OFF THE CHAIN AND JIM CAN GET OUT!

AND UNCLE SILAS HE TRUSTS EVERYBODY!

THERE AIN'T NO WATCHMAN TO BE DRUGGED - NOW THERE OUGHT TO BE A WATCHMAN. THERE AIN'T EVEN A DOG!

AND THERE'S JIM CHAINED BY ONE LEG, WITH A TEN-FOOT CHAIN, TO THE LEG OF HIS BED -

AAAAARGH

JIM COULD A GOT OUT OF THAT WINDOW-HOLE BEFORE THIS, ONLY THERE WOULDN'T BE NO USE TRYING TO TRAVEL WITH A TEN-FOOT CHAIN ON HIS LEG.

WHY, DRAT IT, HUCK, IT'S THE STUPIDEST ARRANGEMENT I EVER SEE.

SPECIALLY WHERE THERE WARN'T ONE OF THEM FURNISHED TO YOU BY THE PEOPLE WHO IT WAS THEIR DUTY TO FURNISH THEM,

ANYHOW, THERE'S ONE THING - THERE'S MORE HONOR IN GETTING HIM OUT THROUGH A LOT OF DIFFICULTIES AND DANGERS.

AND YOU HAD TO CONTRIVE THEM ALL OUT OF YOUR OWN HEAD.

WANT IT FOR JIM TO KEEP A JOURNAL ON.

WHAT DO WE WANT OF A SHIRT, TOM?

WE GOT TO BORROW A SHIRT, TOO.

WE'LL NEED TOOLS TO DIG WITH, TOO. WE AIN'T A-GOING TO GNAW HIM OUT, AFTER ALL.

JOURNAL YOUR GRANNY - JIM CAN'T WRITE.

DID YOU *EVER* HEAR OF A PRISONER HAVING PICKS AND SHOVELS, AND ALL THE MODERN CONVENIENCES IN HIS WARDROBE TO DIG HIMSELF OUT WITH?

AIN'T THEM OLD CRIPPLED PICKS AND THINGS IN THERE GOOD ENOUGH TO DIG A NIGGER OUT WITH?

WELL, THEN, WHAT DO WE WANT?

A COUPLE OF CASE-KNIVES.

YES.

TO DIG THE FOUNDATIONS OUT FROM UNDER THAT CABIN WITH?

IT DON'T MAKE NO DIFFERENCE HOW FOOLISH IT IS, IT'S THE *RIGHT* WAY.

CONFOUND IT, IT'S FOOLISH, TOM.

AND THERE AIN'T NO *OTHER* WAY, THAT EVER I HEARD OF, AND I'VE READ ALL THE BOOKS THAT GIVES ANY INFORMATION ABOUT THESE THINGS.

AND IT'S THE REGULAR WAY.

HOW LONG WILL IT TAKE, TOM?

THIRTY-SEVEN YEARS. THAT'S THE KIND.

THERE'S ONE THING - JIM'S TOO OLD TO BE DUG OUT WITH A CASE-KNIFE. HE WON'T LAST.

YEAH!

HMM...

THEN WE REALLY DIG RIGHT IN, AS QUICK AS WE CAN.

YES.

HMM... WE CAN'T RESK BEING AS LONG DIGGING HIM OUT AS WE OUGHT TO.

AFTER THAT, WE CAN LET ON, TO OURSELVES, THAT WE WAS AT IT THIRTY-SEVEN YEARS.

THEN WE CAN SNATCH HIM OUT AND RUSH HIM AWAY THE FIRST TIME THERE'S AN ALARM. YES, I RECKON THAT 'LL BE THE BEST WAY.

NOW, THERE'S SENSE IN THAT.

LETTING ON DON'T COST NOTHING; LETTING ON AIN'T NO TROUBLE.

327

WE DUG AND DUG WITH THE CASE-KNIVES TILL MOST MIDNIGHT; AND THEN WE WAS DOG-TIRED, AND OUR HANDS WAS BLISTERED, AND YET YOU COULDN'T SEE WE'D DONE ANYTHING HARDLY.

FINALLY I GOT TOM TO SAY THAT WE *COULD* DIG HIM OUT WITH THE PICKS, AND JUST *LET ON* IT'S CASE-KNIVES.

CHAPTER XXXVI TO XXXVIII

THE NEXT NIGHT WE WHIRLED IN WITH THE PICK AND SHOVEL, AND IN ABOUT TWO HOURS AND A HALF THE JOB WAS DONE.

JIM WAS SO GLAD TO SEE US HE MOST CRIED.

HUUUU – UCK...!

HE WAS FOR HAVING US HUNT UP A COLD-CHISEL TO CUT THE CHAIN OFF OF HIS LEG WITH RIGHT AWAY, AND CLEARING OUT WITHOUT LOSING ANY TIME.

BUT TOM HE SHOWED HIM HOW UNREGULAR IT WOULD BE, AND SET DOWN AND TOLD HIM ALL ABOUT OUR PLANS.

HE TOLD JIM HOW WE'D HAVE TO SMUGGLE IN THE LARGE THINGS BY NAT; AND WE WOULD PUT SMALL THINGS IN UNCLE'S COAT-POCKETS AND HE MUST STEAL THEM OUT; AND WE WOULD TIE THINGS TO AUNT'S APRON-STRINGS, IF WE GOT A CHANCE.

JIM HE COULDN'T SEE NO SENSE IN THE MOST OF IT, BUT HE ALLOWED WE WAS WHITE FOLKS AND KNOWED BETTER THAN HIM; SO HE WAS SATISFIED, AND SAID HE WOULD DO IT ALL JUST AS TOM SAID.

WE FOUND A COUPLE OF THINGS THAT WOULD BE HANDY FOR A PRISONER, ONLY AUNT SALLY GOT ALL HOT AND RED AND CROSS BECAUSE SHE COULDN'T FIND ONE OF THE SPOONS, NOR HALF THE CANDLES, NOR NOTHING.

SHE WAS JUST A-BILING, SO WE SLIPPED BACK THE SPOONS WE HAD.

SO WE SMOUCHED A GRINDSTONE FROM THE MILL, AND SET OUT TO ROLL HER HOME.

TOM SAID JIM'D GOT TO WRITE HIS NAME ON THE WALLS; THERE WARN'T NO CASE OF A STATE PRISONER NOT SCRABBLING HIS INSCRIPTION TO LEAVE BEHIND, AND HIS COAT OF ARMS.

BUT THE LOG WALLS WEREN'T A-GOING TO DO; WE HAD TO DIG THE INSCRIPTIONS INTO A ROCK.

IT WAS A MOST NATION TOUGH JOB. SOMETIMES, DO WHAT WE COULD, WE COULDN'T KEEP HER FROM FALLING OVER, AND SHE COME MIGHTY NEAR MASHING US EVERY TIME.

SO HE RAISED UP HIS BED AND SLID THE CHAIN OFF OF THE BED-LEG, AND WRAPT IT ROUND AND ROUND HIS NECK, AND LAID INTO THAT GRINDSTONE.

WE GOT HER THERE; AND THEN WE WAS PLUMB PLAYED OUT, AND MOST DROWNDED WITH SWEAT. WE SEE IT WARN'T NO USE; WE GOT TO GO AND FETCH JIM.

THEN WE HELPED HIM FIX HIS CHAIN BACK ON THE BED-LEG, AND WAS READY FOR BED OURSELVES.

AFTER A WHILE OF THIS, THOUGH, JIM SAID HE WAS BLEST IF HE COULD SEE THE POINT OF ALL THIS.

TOM SAID HE'D GOT TO TAME ANIMALS WITH HIS JEWS-HARP AND GROW FLOWERS WATERED BY HIS TEARS, LIKE ALL THE STATE PRISONERS DONE IN THEIR TIME.

I NEVER KNOWED B'FO' 'T WAS SO MUCH BOTHER AND TROUBLE TO BE A PRISONER!

SO JIM HE WAS SORRY, AND SAID HE WOULDN'T BEHAVE SO NO MORE, AND THEN ME AND TOM SHOVED FOR BED.

TOM MOST LOST ALL PATIENCE WITH HIM; SAID HE WAS JUST LOADENED DOWN WITH MORE GAUDIER CHANCES THAN A PRISONER EVER HAD IN THE WORLD TO MAKE A NAME FOR HIMSELF, AND THEY WAS JUST ABOUT WASTED ON HIM.

SCRIT SCRIT

CHAPTER XXIX

THREE WEEKS LATER

THIS MORNING THE OLD MAN ALLOWED HE WOULD ADVERTISE JIM IN THE ST. LOUIS AND NEW ORLEANS PAPERS; WE HAIN'T GOT NO TIME TO LOSE.

WELL, TIME FOR THE NONNAMOUS LETTERS.

SCRIT SCRIT

WHAT'S THEM?

WARNINGS TO THE PEOPLE THAT SOMETHING IS UP.

BUT LOOKY HERE TOM, WHAT DO WE WANT TO WARN ANYBODY FOR THAT SOMETHING'S UP? LET THEM FIND IT OUT FOR THEMSELVES – IT'S THEIR LOOK-OUT.

YES, I KNOW; BUT YOU CAN'T DEPEND ON THEM.

IT'S THE WAY THEY'VE ACTED FROM THE VERY START – LEFT US TO DO *EVERYTHING*.

THEY'RE SO CONFIDING AND MULLET-HEADED THEY DON'T TAKE NOTICE OF NOTHING AT ALL.

SO AFTER ALL OUR HARD WORK AND TROUBLE THIS ESCAPE 'LL GO OFF PERFECTLY FLAT; WON'T AMOUNT TO NOTHING – WON'T BE NOTHING TO IT.

IF WE DON'T *GIVE* THEM NOTICE THERE WON'T BE NOBODY NOR NOTHING TO INTERFERE WITH US!

WELL, AS FOR ME, TOM, THAT'S THE WAY I'D LIKE.

BUT I AIN'T GOING TO MAKE NO COMPLAINT. ANY WAY THAT SUITS YOU SUITS ME.

SHUCKS!

ALL RIGHT!

SCRIT SCRIT

SO TOM HE WROTE A NONNAMOUS LETTER, AND I SHOVED IT UNDER THE FRONT DOOR THAT NIGHT.

NEXT NIGHT WE STUCK A PICTURE OF A SKULL AND CROSSBONES ON THE FRONT DOOR, AND NEXT, FOR THE GRAND BULGE, A LETTER ABOUT A DESPRATE GANG OF CUTTHROATS GOING TO STEAL THE RUNAWAY NIGGER.

WELL, THEY WAS ALL IN SUCH A SWEAT AND WORRY THEY DIDN'T KNOW WHICH END THEY WAS STANDING ON, AND THEY MADE US GO RIGHT OFF TO BED THE MINUTE WE WAS DONE SUPPER.

FMP

CHAPTER XL

AS SOON AS WE WAS HALF UP STAIRS WE SLID FOR THE CELLAR CUPBOARD...

MURMUR

MURMUR

MURMUR

MY, BUT THERE WAS A CROWD THERE!

FIFTEEN FARMERS; AND EVERY ONE OF THEM HAD A GUN...

NO! – IS THAT SO? AIN'T IT BULLY?

THE HOUSE IS FULL OF MEN, YONDER, WITH GUNS!

WHY, HUCK, IF IT WAS TO DO OVER AGAIN, I BET I COULD FETCH TWO HUNDRED!

TOM, WE MUST JUMP FOR IT NOW, NOT A MOMENT TO LOSE!

RIGHT AT YOUR ELBOW! HE'S DRESSED, AND EVERYTHING'S READY.

IF WE COULD PUT IT OFF TILL –

!?

HURRY! HURRY! WHERE'S JIM?

THAT'S RIGHT, THE YALLER WENCH'S FROCK...

NOW WE'LL SLIDE OUT AND GIVE THE SHEEP-SIGNAL.

I'LL STUFF JIM'S CLOTHES FULL OF STRAW AND LAY IT ON HIS BED, AND JIM 'LL TAKE THIS NIGGER WOMAN'S GOWN AND WEAR IT!

WE'LL ALL EVADE TOGETHER!

STEP
STEP STEP

JIM MOST REFUSED, BUT IN THE END TOM GOT IT ON HIM.

HUSTLE!

THEY'VE COME TO THE DOOR ALREADY!

I *TOLD* YOU WE'D BE TOO SOON; THEY HAVEN'T COME - THE DOOR IS LOCKED.

CLATTER

BUT WE GOT UNDER ALL RIGHT, HUCK.

THEY'RE GONNA COME INTO THE CABIN!

SCREEEEE

YOU LAY FOR 'EM IN THE DARK AND KILL 'EM WHEN THEY COME!

CAN'T MAKE THE LEAST NOISE...

GOT TO GET TO THE RIVER!

THE REST OF YOU SCATTER AROUND A PIECE, AND LISTEN IF YOU CAN HEAR 'EM COMING.

WE GOT TO THE FENCE ALL RIGHT, AND ME AND JIM OVER IT.

WHUMP

ERRRGH...

SNAP!

!!

WHO'S THAT?

HERE THEY ARE!

ANSWER, OR I'LL SHOOT!

...

AFTER 'EM, BOYS!

BANG!

THEY'VE BROKE FOR THE RIVER!

BANG!

BANG!

BANG!

BANG!

HURRY!

ZIP

ON MY WAY!

!

BOYS, WE DONE IT ELEGANT!

HUF HUF HUF

NOW, OLD JIM, YOU'RE A FREE MAN AGAIN, AND I BET YOU WON'T EVER BE A SLAVE NO MORE.

EN A MIGHTY GOOD JOB IT WUZ, TOO HUCK. EN DAY AIN'T NOBODY KIN GIT UP A PLAN DAT'S MO' MIXED-UP EN SPLENDID DEN WHAT DAT ONE WUZ.

HA HA HA

... TOM?

WHAT AN EVASION! DONE IT JUST AS SLICK AS NOTHING AT ALL!

I GOT A BULLET IN MY LEG, AND THAT'S JUST HOW AN ESCAPE OUGHT TO GO!

MY CALF – OUCH! IT HURTS CONSIDERABLE!

WHERE IS IT? DOES IT HURT?

YOU WERE SHOT?!

GIMME THE RAGS; I CAN DO IT MYSELF.

JIM, TEAR UP THAT SHIRT OF THE DUKE'S FOR TO BANDAGE HIM UP!

YES!

...

DON'T STOP NOW, AND THE EVASION BOOMING ALONG SO HANDSOME; MAN THE SWEEPS, AND SET HER LOOSE!

WELL, DEN DIS IS DE WAY IT LOOK TO ME, HUCK.

SAY IT, JIM.

EF IT WUZ *HIM* DAT 'UZ BEIN' SOT FREE, EN ONE ER DE BOYS WUZ TO GIT SHOT, WOULD HE SAY, 'GO ON EN SAVE ME, NEMMINE 'BOUT A DOCTOR F'R TO SAVE DIS ONE?'

IS DAT LIKE MARS TOM SAWYER? WOULD HE SAY DAT?

YOU *BET* HE WOULDN'T!

WELL, DEN, IS JIM GYWNE TO SAY IT?

NO, SAH – !

I DOAN' BUDGE A STEP OUT'N DIS PLACE 'DOUT A DOCTOR, NOT IF IT'S FORTY YEAR!

NO, SAH, I AIN'T GWYNE TO.

JIM, MAN THE SWEEPS! DON'T FOOL AROUND HERE!

...

I KNOWED HE WAS WHITE INSIDE, AND I RECKONED HE'D SAY WHAT HE DID SAY — SO IT WAS ALL RIGHT NOW.

I TOLD TOM I WAS A-GOING FOR A DOCTOR. HE RAISED CONSIDERABLE ROW ABOUT IT, BUT IT DIDN'T DO NO GOOD.

HE GIVE US A PIECE OF HIS MIND, BUT ME AND JIM STUCK TO IT AND WOULDN'T BUDGE.

JUST GO

WHY

NO

ARGH

347

SO I LEFT, AND JIM WAS TO HIDE IN THE WOODS WHEN HE SEE THE DOCTOR COMING TILL HE WAS GONE AGAIN.

CHAPTER XLI

THE DOCTOR WAS AN OLD MAN; A VERY NICE, KIND-LOOKING OLD MAN WHEN I GOT HIM UP.

BUT WHEN HE SEES THE CANOE HE DIDN'T LIKE THE LOOK OF HER - SAID SHE WAS BIG ENOUGH FOR ONE, BUT DIDN'T LOOK PRETTY SAFE FOR TWO.

NEXT TIME I WAKED UP THE SUN WAS AWAY UP OVER MY HEAD!

I SAYS TO MYSELF, I'LL WAIT, AND MAKE SURE HE CAN'T LET THE CAT OUT OF THE BAG, SO I GOT SOME SLEEP...

SO I TOLD HIM JUST HOW TO FIND THE RAFT, AND THEN HE STARTED.

348

I SHOT OUT AND WENT FOR THE DOCTOR'S HOUSE, BUT THEY TOLD ME HE'D GONE AWAY IN THE NIGHT SOME TIME OR OTHER, AND WARN'T BACK YET.

WELL, THINKS I, THAT LOOKS POWERFUL BAD FOR TOM, AND I'LL DIG OUT FOR THE ISLAND RIGHT OFF.

SO AWAY I SHOVED, AND TURNED THE CORNER, AND NEARLY RAMMED MY HEAD INTO UNCLE SILAS'S STOMACH! I TOLD HIM SID WAS LAYING UP AT THE POST OFFICE TO SEE WHAT HE COULD HEAR ABOUT THE RUNAWAY NIGGER.

BUT JUST AS I SUSPICIONED, TOM WARN'T THERE.

I COULDN'T GET HIM TO LET ME STAY AND WAIT FOR SID; AND HE SAID THERE WARN'T NO USE IN IT, AND I MUST COME ALONG, AND LET AUNT SALLY SEE WE WAS ALL RIGHT.

WHEN WE GOT HOME AUNT SALLY WAS THAT GLAD TO SEE ME SHE LAUGHED AND CRIED BOTH, AND HUGGED ME, AND GIVE ME ONE OF THEM LICKINGS OF HERN THAT DON'T AMOUNT TO SHUCKS.

HUGGG

LOOK AT THAT-AIR GRINDSTONE, S'I! SCRABBLIN' ALL THEM CRAZY THINGS!

AND THAT-AIR LADDER MADE OUT'N RAGS! 'N' WHO DUG THAT-AIR HOLE?

AND THE PLACE WAS PLUM FULL OF FARMERS AND FARMERS' WIVES, TO DINNER; AND SUCH ANOTHER CLACK A BODY NEVER HEARD.

I B'LIEVE THE NIGGER WAS CRAZY.

THEY THOUGH JIM MUST HAVE HAD A POWERFUL LOT OF HELP, AND THEY THOUGHT IT THROUGH AND RECKONED IT MUST A BEEN SPIRITS THAT HELPED HIM, SINCE NO ONE EVER CAUGHT HIDE NOR HAIR OF THE THIEVES.

THEY WAS MOST AFEARED TO LIVE THEREABOUTS, WITH SPIRITS AND HOUSE-THIEVES ABOUT!

UNCLE SILAS COME BACK ABOUT TEN A LITTLE BIT UNEASY; HADN'T RUN ACROSS TOM'S TRACK. AUNT SALLY WAS A GOOD *DEAL* UNEASY.

SHE MOTHERED ME SO GOOD I FELT MEAN, AND LIKE I COULDN'T LOOK HER IN THE FACE.

WHEN I WENT UP TO BED SHE COME UP WITH ME, AND TUCKED ME IN.

THE DOOR AIN'T GOING TO BE LOCKED, TOM, AND THERE'S THE WINDOW AND THE ROD;

BUT YOU'LL BE GOOD, WON'T YOU? AND YOU WON'T GO? FOR MY SAKE.

AND WHEN SHE WAS GOING AWAY SHE LOOKED DOWN IN MY EYES SO STEADY AND GENTLE, AND SAYS:

LAWS KNOWS I *WANTED* TO GO BAD ENOUGH TO SEE ABOUT TOM, AND WAS ALL INTENDING TO GO; BUT AFTER THAT I WOULDN'T A WENT, NOT FOR KINGDOMS.

BUT THE NEXT MORNING THE DOCTOR BRUNG TOM SAWYER HOME ANYWAY.

OH, HE'S DEAD, HE'S DEAD, I KNOW HE'S DEAD!

CHAPTER XXLII

...IT'S THE PERFECT... PERFECT EVASION... LOUIS... SIXTEENTH...

351

WELL, HE AIN'T IN HIS RIGHT MIND, BUT HE'S ALIVE.

HE'S ALIVE, THANK GOD! AND THAT'S ENOUGH!

!

THIS NIGGER OUGHT TO BE HUNG FOR MAKING SUCH A RAFT OF TROUBLE!

HANG HIM AS AN EXAMPLE TO THE OTHERS!

HIS OWNER'LL TURN UP AND MAKE US PAY FOR HIM, SURE.

IT WON'T ANSWER AT ALL. HE AIN'T OUR NIGGER.

DON'T BE NO ROUGHER ON HIM THAN YOU'RE OBLEEGED TO.

HE AIN'T NO BAD NIGGER, GENTLEMEN; THAT'S WHAT I THINK ABOUT HIM.

DOCTOR?

EH?

WHEN I GOT TO WHERE I FOUND THE BOY I SEE I COULDN'T CUT THE BULLET OUT WITHOUT SOME HELP.

HE WARN'T IN NO CONDITION FOR ME TO LEAVE TO GO AND GET HELP;

AND HE GOT A LITTLE WORSE AND A LITTLE WORSE, AND AFTER A LONG TIME HE WENT OUT OF HIS HEAD.

SO I SAYS, I GOT TO HAVE HELP SOMEHOW.

AND THE MINUTE I SAYS IT OUT CRAWLS THIS NIGGER FROM SOMEWHERES AND SAYS HE'LL HELP.

AND HE DONE IT, TOO, AND DONE IT VERY WELL.

I HAD A COUPLE OF PATIENTS WITH THE CHILLS, AND OF COURSE I'D OF LIKED TO RUN UP TO TOWN AND SEE THEM.

OF COURSE I JUDGED HE MUST BE A RUNAWAY NIGGER. IT WAS A FIX, I TELL YOU!

BUT I DASN'T, BECAUSE THE NIGGER MIGHT GET AWAY, AND THEN I'D BE TO BLAME.

AND YET NEVER A SKIFF COME CLOSE ENOUGH FOR ME TO HAIL.

I NEVER SEE A NIGGER THAT WAS A BETTER NUSS OR FAITH-FULLER.

SO THERE I HAD TO STICK PLUMB UNTIL DAYLIGHT THIS MORNING.

HE WAS RISKING HIS FREEDOM TO DO IT, AND WAS ALL TIRED OUT, TOO. I LIKED THE NIGGER FOR THAT.

I TELL YOU, GENTLEMEN, A NIGGER LIKE THAT IS WORTH A THOUSAND DOLLARS - AND KIND TREATMENT, TOO.

THE OTHERS SOFTENED UP A LITTLE AT THAT.

I WAS MIGHTY THANKFUL TO THAT OLD DOCTOR FOR DOING JIM THAT GOOD TURN.

HMM?

HELLO! – WHY, I'M AT *HOME!* HOW'S THAT? WHERE'S THE RAFT?

IT'S ALL RIGHT.

AND JIM?

THE SAME.

WHY ABOUT THE WAY THE WHOLE THING WAS DONE; HOW WE SET THE RUNAWAY NIGGER FREE - ME AND TOM.

GOOD! SPLENDID! NOW WE'RE ALL RIGHT AND SAFE! DID YOU TELL AUNTY?

WE LAID OUT TO DO IT, AND WE *DONE* IT. AND WE DONE IT ELEGANT, TOO!

ABOUT WHAT, SID?

...

HE'D GOT A START, AND SHE NEVER CHECKED HIM UP, JUST SET AND STARED AND STARED, AND LET HIM CLIP ALONG, AND I SEE IT WARN'T NO USE FOR *ME* TO PUT IN.

- AND WE DONE IT ALL BY OURSELVES, AND *WASN'T* IT BULLY, AUNTY!

YOU JUST GET WELL ONCE, YOU YOUNG SCAMP, AND I LAY I'LL TAN THE OLD HARRY OUT O' BOT O' YE!

OHHHH

SO IT WAS YOU, YOU LITTLE RAPSCALLIONS, THAT'S BEEN MAKING ALL THIS TROUBLE!

AND MIND I TELL YOU IF I CATCH YOU MEDDLING WITH HIM AGAIN —

MEDDLING WITH WHO?

TOM, DIDN'T YOU JUST TELL ME HE WAS ALL RIGHT? HASN'T HE GOT AWAY?

WITH WHO? WHY, THE RUNAWAY NIGGER, OF COURSE.

'DEED HE HASN'T. THEY'VE GOT HIM BACK, SAFE AND SOUND.

HE'S IN THAT CABIN AGAIN, ON BREAD AND WATER, TILL HE'S CLAIMED OR SOLD!

HE AIN'T NO SLAVE - HE'S AS FREE AS ANY CRETUR THAT WALKS THIS EARTH!

WHAT DOES THE CHILD MEAN?

THEY HAIN'T NO *RIGHT* TO SHUT HIM UP!

I MEAN EVERY WORD I SAY, AUNT SALLY!

SHOVE! - AND DON'T YOU LOSE A MINUTE.

IF SOMEBODY DON'T GO, I'LL GO.

I'VE KNOWED HIM ALL HIS LIFE, AND SO HAS TOM, THERE.

OLD MISS WATSON DIED TWO MONTHS AGO, AND SHE WAS ASHAMED THAT SHE WAS EVER GOING TO SELL HIM DOWN THE RIVER, AND SAID SO.

SHE SET HIM FREE IN HER WILL!

360

TOM SAWYER HAD GONE AND TOOK ALL THAT TROUBLE AND BOTHER TO SET A FREE NIGGER FREE!

AND I COULDN'T EVER UNDERSTAND BEFORE, UNTIL THAT MINUTE AND THAT TALK, HOW HE *COULD* HELP A BODY SET A NIGGER FREE WITH HIS BRINGING-UP.

HAH

THEN WHAT ON EARTH DID *YOU* WANT TO SET HIM FREE FOR, SEEING HE WAS ALREADY FREE?

WELL, THAT *IS* A QUESTION, I MUST SAY!

WHY, I WANTED THE *ADVENTURE* OF IT; AND I'D A WADED NECK-DEEP IN BLOOD TO —

HA HA HA HA

IS THAT SO?

AUNT POLLY

GOODNESS ALIVE, AUNT POLLY!

IF TOM'S AUNT POLLY WARN'T STANDING RIGHT THERE, COME ALL THE WAY FROM MISSOURI, I WISH I MAY NEVER!

SISTER! WHY, I DIDN'T EXPECT —

ONE MINUTE, SALLY.

YES, YOU *BETTER* TURN Y'R HEAD AWAY - I WOULD IF I WAS YOU, TOM.

WHY, THAT AIN'T *TOM* - THAT'S SID.

TOM'S - TOM'S - WHY, WHERE IS TOM? HE WAS HERE A MINUTE AGO.

YOU MEAN WHERE'S HUCK *FINN* - THAT'S WHAT YOU MEAN!

I RECKON I HAIN'T RAISED SUCH A SCAMP AS MY TOM ALL THESE YEARS NOT TO KNOW HIM WHEN I *SEE* HIM. THAT *WOULD* BE A PRETTY HOWDY-DO.

SHUFFLE

SHUFFLE

COME OUT FROM UNDER THAT BED, HUCK FINN.

...

SO I DONE IT. BUT NOT FEELING BRASH.

HE HE EH

AUNT SALLY SHE WAS ONE OF THE MIXED-UPEST-LOOKING PERSONS I EVER SEE. SO TOM'S AUNT POLLY, SHE TOLD ALL ABOUT WHO I WAS, AND WHAT.

I HAD TO UP AND TELL HOW I WAS IN SUCH A TIGHT PLACE THAT WHEN MRS. PHELPS TOOK ME FOR TOM SAWYER I HAD TO STAND IT – THERE WARN'T NO OTHER WAY.

I KNOWED HE WOULDN'T MIND, BECAUSE IT WOULD BE NUTS FOR HIM, BEING A MYSTERY, AND HE'D MAKE AN ADVENTURE OUT OF IT, AND BE PERFECTLY SATISFIED.

AUNT POLLY SAID THAT WHEN AUNT SALLY WROTE TO HER THAT TOM AND SID HAD COME ALL RIGHT AND SAFE, SHE KNOWED THAT SHE MIGHT HAVE EXPECTED THAT KIND OF TROUBLE FROM TOM.

TOM HAD GRABBED HER LETTERS AND HIDDEN THEM AWAY, BECAUSE HE KNEW THEY'D JUST MAKE TROUBLE.

SHE WROTE AND WROTE AND DIDN'T GET NO ANSWER, SO SHE HAD TO GO AND TRAPSE ALL THE WAY DOWN THE RIVER TO FIND OUT WHAT HE WAS UP TO *THIS* TIME.

SEVERAL WEEKS LATER

I *TOLE* YOU I BEN RICH WUNST, EN GWINETER TO BE RICH *AGIN;* EN IT'S COME TRUE; EN HEAH SHE IS!

CHAPTER THE LAST

TOM GIVE HIM FORTY DOLLARS FOR BEING PRISONER FOR US SO PATIENT, AND DOING IT UP SO GOOD...

LE'S ALL THREE SLIDE OUT OF HERE ONE OF THESE NIGHTS AND GET AN OUTFIT, AND GO FOR HOWLING ADVENTURES AMONGST THE INJUNS, OVER IN THE TERRITORY!

ALL RIGHT, THAT SUITS ME, BUT I AIN'T GOT NO MONEY FOR TO BUY THE OUTFIT.

IT'S LIKELY PAP'S BEEN BACK BEFORE NOW, AND GOT IT ALL AWAY FROM JUDGE THATCHER AND DRUNK IT UP.

NO, HE HAIN'T, IT'S ALL THERE YET - AND YOUR PAP HAIN'T EVER BEEN BACK SINCE. HADN'T WHEN I COME AWAY, ANYHOW.

WHY, JIM?

HE AIN'T A-COMIN' BACK NO MO', HUCK.

NEMMINE WHY, HUCK - BUT HE AIN'T COMIN' BACK NO MO.

DOAN' YOU MEMBER DE HOUSE DAT WAS FLOAT'N DOWN DE RIVER?

TELL ME!

I KEPT AT HIM.

DEY WUZ A MAN IN DAH, KIVERED UP, EN I WENT IN EN UNKIVERED HIM AND DIDN' LET YOU COME IN?

WELL, DEN, YOU KIN GIT YO' MONEY WHEN YOU WANTS IT, KAZE DAT WUZ HIM.

...

TOM'S MOST WELL NOW.

SO THERE AIN'T NOTHING MORE TO WRITE ABOUT, AND I AM ROTTEN GLAD OF IT.

IF I'D A KNOWED WHAT A TROUBLE IT WAS TO MAKE A BOOK I WOULDN'T A TACKLED IT, AND AIN'T A-GOING TO NO MORE.

SHUF

THUMP

THUMP!

SCUFF

SCUFF

SCUFF

AUNT SALLY SHE'S GOING TO ADOPT ME AND SIVILIZE ME.

I CAN'T STAND IT. I BEEN THERE BEFORE.

I RECKON I GOT TO LIGHT OUT FOR THE TERRITORY.

THE END.

YOURS TRULY,
HUCK FINN.

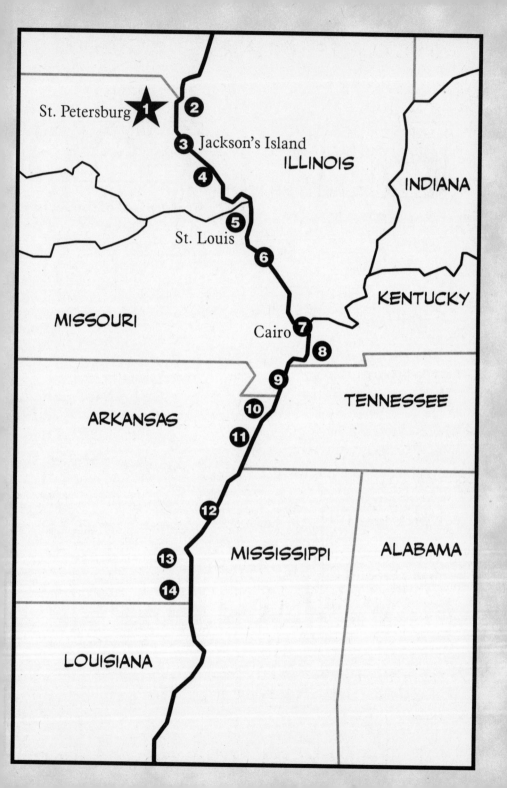

HUCKLEBERRY FINN'S JOURNEY

 1 St. Petersburg, MO (Hannibal)

2 Pap's Cabin

3 Jackson's Island, MO (Glasscock's Island) - met up with the ran-away Jim.

4 The Floating House - found the dead body.

5 St. Louis - Mrs. Judith Loftus' home.

6 The Wrecked Steamboat - met 3 mysterious men.

7 Cairo, IL - met Parker and John., then raft got hit by boat.

8 Grangerfords VS Shepherdsons

9 The Arrival of the King and the Duke.

10 Camp Meeting

11 Boggs' shooting

12 Learned about the Wilks funeral

13 The Wilks' House

14 The Phelps' Farm

A KUMA THEATRE

I'M SO GLAD TO SEE EVERYONE HERE~ FIRST LET ME SAY...

HELLO, EVERYONE! I'M THE ARTIST THAT DREW THIS BOOK — MY NAME IS KUMA~

I'M BUNNY, GIVING KUMA A HARD TIME~

THANK YOU BOSSES FOR GIVING ME THE OPPORTUNITY TO DRAW *HUCK FINN*!

DON'T ASSUME THE READERS HAVE **YOUR** BAD HABITS!

DO NOT TURN TO THIS WRITEUP FIRST!

YOU SHOULD READ THE BOOK FROM THE BEGINNING!

BY THE WAY, THE WORKS OF MR. MARK TWAIN ARE REALLY SPLENDID! HE EVEN TOOK CARE OF PARTS THAT AREN'T MENTIONED IN THE STORY~

HOW SO?

OH! *TOM SAWYER* IS ALSO IN THE WORKS, SO PLEASE SUPPORT IT IF YOU HAVE A FEW EXTRA BUCKS IN YOUR POCKET~

SPECIAL THANKS TO THE SCRIPT WRITER, THE EDITOR, AND ALL THE ASSISTANTS —

THE BOOK WOULDN'T EXIST WITHOUT ALL OF YOU~

AND YOUR POINT BEING?

AND WHEN THE END OF THE STORY COMES, I CAN CONNECT ALL THOSE THOUGHTS TOGETHER!

SO WHILE I WORK, I OCCASIONALLY HAVE THOUGHTS ABOUT "WHAT DID THIS CHARACTER DO OR WANT TO DO AT THIS MOMENT?"...

RECENTLY I'VE BECOME A FAN OF ENSEMBLE DRAMAS,

SO WHAT'S YOUR THEORY... ?

......

AND THAT SOMEONE WAS THE SECOND SISTER, SUSAN!

THEIR TIMING WAS JUST WAY TOO CONVENIENT! IT WAS LIKE SOMEONE INTENTIONALLY ARRANGED IT.

WELL, LIKE, IN THE STORY ABOUT THE THREE SISTERS, I BELIEVED THAT THE SECOND HARVEY AND WILLIAM WERE ALSO FAKES.

Editor's Note: This is 100% KUMA's own speculation!

......

AND THE PROOF IS... ?

2. Susan thought that it might be dangerous to confirm these suspicions on her own, so she asked her sister Joanna to talk to Huck and see what he had to say.

1. During the banquet, Dr. Robinson accused the King and the Duke of being fakes, which raised Susan's suspicions.

DUE TO LIMITED SPACE, I'LL EXPLAIN WITH THIS FLOWCHART:

3. Susan told Joanna that Huck would know how things were in England, so it might be easier to start by talking with him about his life or his work.

4. Susan then hid outside the door and eavesdropped on their conversation! Mary Jane interrupted that talk, but Susan was able to confirm that Huck didn't know anything about England and was lying.

6. The two of them gathered evidence while awaiting the real uncles.

5. After Susan was sure that the King and the Duke were frauds, she went to Dr. Robinson for help.

7. But then the King and the Duke proposed taking the sisters to England, at which point Susan realized that she was out of time...

8. So Dr. Robinson found two people to act as the sisters' uncles, and even though things got very bad, they were still able to reveal the frauds.

HM...IT KINDA MAKES SENSE - AND IT DOESN'T CONFLICT WITH THE ORIGINAL STORY MUCH.

I HAVE THIS THEORY FOR A SIDE STORY ABOUT MARY JANE, FROM THE DAY SHE LEFT THE HOUSE TO THE DAY OF THE AUCTION...

MARY JANE SUDDENLY MOVED OUT AND LEFT SUSAN AND JOANNA AT HOME!

HOWEVER, WHEN THEY WERE PREPARING FOR THE AUCTION, SOMETHING UNEXPECTED HAPPENED!

60 MORE PAGES...

LEAVE THESE IMAGININGS TO YOUR OWN DOUJINSHI-!!

THERE'S MORE?

YOU'RE RIGHT..

SOME DAY, IF WE MEET UP, WE WILL CROSS CHECK OUR ANSWERS~

BYE!!

THERE'S NOT ENOUGH SPACE HERE, IF YOU ARE INTERESTED, TRY THINKING ABOUT WHAT HAPPENED IN ORDER TO ALLOW JIM TO MAKE HIS ESCAPE!

I ALSO HAVE A THEORY ABOUT THE MONTH THAT HUCK SPENT WITH HIS FATHER AFTER BEING KIDNAPPED~

The King

The Duke

Paps

Uncle Silas Phelps

KUMA'S SKETCH BOOK - GUYS

Tom

Huck

Jim

Judith Loftus

Aunt Sally

COVER & PIN-UP
IDEA SKETCHES

KUMA'S SKETCH BOOK - GIRLS

Susan

Mary Jane

Joanna

I RECKON I'M TO BLAME!

I JUDGED I OUGHT TO TOLD MISS SOPHIA'S FATHER ABOUT THAT PAPER AND THE CURIOUS WAY SHE ACTED, AND THEN MAYBE HE WOULD A LOCKED HER UP, AND THIS AWFUL MESS WOULDN'T EVER HAPPENED.

HE WAS MIGHTY GOOD TO ME!

THAT WAS BUCK, KILT, WITH HIS FACE ALL COVERED UP...

SENSITIVE OR DISTURBING SCENES:

As 'keeping the story intact' was the priority of our adaptations, what should I do when working on disturbing topics? I talked to KUMA, the artist, about how to solve this problem by using the natural advantages of illustration. For example, in Pikesville the King and the Duke are punished for their crimes by being tarred and feathered before being run out of town on a rail – an extremely painful punishment that is also meant to cause great shame. This scene couldn't be removed without also removing the end of the con men's story, which wouldn't work at all! Therefore, I persuaded KUMA to keep this part, and we decided to show the scene in silhouette to soften the image and remove the more disturbing aspects, and this seemed like a good compromise.

IT WAS A DREADFUL THING TO SEE. HUMAN BEINGS CAN BE AWFUL CRUEL TO ONE ANOTHER.

RAAAAAAR

AS THEY WENT BY I SEE THEY HAD THE KING AND THE DUKE ASTRADDLE OF A RAIL – THEY WAS ALL OVER TAR AND FEATHERS, AND DIDN'T LOOK LIKE NOTHING IN THE WORLD THAT WAS HUMAN.

BOOOO

SOLD

GET 'EM

Continues on Page 3...

CRYSTAL S. CHAN:
ADAPTING HUCK FINN

Mark Twain's **ADVENTURES OF HUCKLEBERRY FINN** is a biting satire and a criticism of the time period in which it takes place. Nothing like it had ever been written before, and it was hugely controversial at the time - it remains controversial even today. Race, religion, human nature, human foolishness: these subjects and more are scrutinized. Nothing is spared. The aim of *MANGA CLASSICS* is to create a manga version of each story that is as close to the original author's work as possible. Those topics – those controversies – are the backbone of the story, and I did my best to fit them all into the space provided. Here's how I did it:

PRIORITY - KEEPING ALL THE STORY POINTS:

Although *ADVENTURES OF HUCKLEBERRY FINN* is a sequel to *THE ADVENTURES OF TOM SAWYER*, its story structure is very different. *TOM SAWYER* sticks close to Tom's hometown and the things that happened there; *HUCKLEBERRY FINN* follows Huck and Jim for miles down the Mississippi River, touching on their interactions with the locals in each new place. The story is much bigger, but few of the locations have any bearing on each other beyond what Huck learns from them. Compared to other *MANGA CLASSICS* titles, it would have been easy to cut down the plot – entire locations could have been removed without damaging the overall story. For example, during production, some of our crew thought that the story of the Grangerford-Shepherdson feud was not interesting enough to keep. However, the aim of *MANGA CLASSICS* is to be faithful to the original book, so I preferred to keep the story and compress the details instead.

Moreover, I believe that Huck's time with the Grangerfords has quite a lot of influence on him. The deaths caused by the feud help him to realize that the ways of civilized society are not always absolutely right. That realization, along with his other experiences along the Mississippi, helps Huck to eventually break with his faltering moral code and act according to his conscience instead, moving to rescue Jim after the King turns him in for the reward.

'Not being interesting enough' was definitely another problem. When I compressed the Grangerford plot I also moved the foreshadowing to a different spot on the timeline, to allow Huck to realize that something was going on between Sophia and Harney before they run away together and trigger the final fight between their families. Not only did this allow me to keep the story intact, but it made the climax develop in a way more suited to the manga format.

WORKING WITH MR. KUMA:

Since this story is told entirely from Huck's point of view, a lot of things that happen in it are never fully explained, since Huck doesn't know or understand some things. This left a lot up to the reader's imagination – and to KUMA's! When we talked about the story KUMA would often guess at the motivation of the other characters, wondering about their stories. A lot of his ideas were really interesting, but since we needed to stay loyal to the original book, we couldn't use them. I hope KUMA will be able to make use of his storytelling talent in future books!

RANDOM THOUGHTS:

When Tom talks about his plan to save Jim, one of the books he mentions taking inspiration from is *THE COUNT OF MONTE CRISTO*. If you've also read the *MANGA CLASSICS* version of that book, you'll find that Jim's odd 'escape' does mirror the Count's escape in several ways!

You may have noticed that the King and the Duke make an attempt to put on two Shakespeare plays, *ROMEO AND JULIET* and *HAMLET* – their versions of these two plays are completely wrong. They're making up the stories based on what little they remember, and they don't remember them well at all. We here at *MANGA CLASSICS* plan to release manga versions of both these plays in the future, and we guarantee that WE won't mess them up!

I have always believed that 'all men are created equal'. It is my wish that there be no more slavery in the world, and that everyone can look on everyone else as equals. I hope through Mark Twain's work here, we can learn something about equality in life, and how people of color were treated back in the days. As for the various controversial words and ideas in the story, I will leave the final judgment on them up to you, the reader.

Adapting one of the "Great American Novels" is not an easy task. I wish to make sure that the story is loyal to the original text, while I also needed to make sure that the story flowed smoothly and read well in graphic novel form. All the original plot points were included, and I hope my changes are subtle enough that it's difficult to spot the places where I made amendments without looking at the original book. If that is the case after you have read the book, then I think I have succeeded in adapting the story! Thank you very much for your support!

If you'd like to share your thoughts with me, please email me at CRYSTAL@MANGACLASSICS.COM

Crystal (Silvermoon) Chan

...Continued from Page 2

FITTING EVERYTHING INTO ONE VOLUME:

Although we do not have a strict limit in our production, page count in our manga version is still relatively limited, as we wish to keep it within the 350 - 400 page range per book. With that in mind, we have to made a few adjustments to the storytelling in order to fit all the story points in our adaptation. For example, when Huck was living with the Grangerfords and went with Jack to see the water moccasins, I made him use this time to recall Sophia asking him to retrieve her Bible after going to church with her family.

It's pretty common to use 'flashbacks' to combine the scenes, and I was able to blend Huck's thoughts and feelings into one section. It makes it easier for the reader to understand Huck's thoughts while making sure that they have the same blind spots as Huck does. This adds to the foreshadowing without revealing everything ahead of time.

Another way to save space involves estimating the required page count beforehand. If we have too many pages, the scene will need to be rewritten shorter while still maintaining the plot and characters. As I wouldn't cut out any of the plot, I could only adjust the details! For example, near the beginning of the book when Tom comes to the Douglas house to fetch Huck, Tom insists that Huck come to the kitchen with him right under the nose of the sleeping Jim, as an additional adventure. In the our version I made Tom go alone, dismissing it with a single panel and line of dialogue. This act of Tom seems like a minor detail, but I didn't wish to remove that part entirely because it shows the readers what Tom is like - this is his very first appearance in the book, and he's one of the main characters, so it's very important to show his adventurous side early on!

ONE SMALL OMISSION:

I believe it's clear now how hard I worked to keep the plot intact, but there's one detail that was omitted. In the original book Huck often smoked tobacco and would go ashore to buy it; this bad habit showing to strengthened Huck's image as a bad kid. He doesn't smoke in the *MANGA CLASSICS* adaptation because we don't want to encourage this harmful habits!

Manga Classics:
Pride and Prejudice
Hard Cover $24.99
ISBN #978-1-927925-17-1
Soft Cover $17.99
ISBN #978-1-927-925-18-8

Manga Classics:
Emma
Hard Cover $24.99
ISBN #978-1-927925-36-2
Soft Cover $17.99
ISBN #978-1-927-925-35-5

Manga Classics:
Sense and Sensibility
Hard Cover $24.99
ISBN #978-1-927925-62-1
Soft Cover $17.99
ISBN #978-1-927925-63-8

Manga Classics:
Jane Austen Coloring Book
Soft Cover $12.99
ISBN #978-1-927925-78-2

Manga Classics:
The Scarlet Letter
Hard Cover $24.99
ISBN #978-1-927925-34-8
Soft Cover $17.99
ISBN #978-1-927925-33-1

Manga Classics:
Jane Eyre
Hard Cover $24.99
ISBN #978-1-927925-64-5
Soft Cover $17.99
ISBN #978-1-927925-65-2

Manga Classics:
The Jungle Book
Hard Cover $24.99
ISBN #978-1-772940-18-3
Soft Cover $17.99
ISBN #978-1-772940-19-0

Manga Classics:
Les Miserables
Hard Cover $24.99
ISBN #978-1-927925-15-7
Soft Cover $17.99
ISBN #978-1-927925-16-4

Manga Classics:
Great Expectations
Hard Cover $24.99
ISBN #978-1-927925-32-4
Soft Cover $17.99
ISBN #978-1-927925-31-7